SELF-CARE
FOR WITCHES

A Magical Collection of Activities and Tools for Well-Being, with Crystals, Herbs, Oils, Divination Techniques, and Spells

LISA CHAMBERLAIN & KIKI DOMBROWSKI

Self-Care for Witches

Copyright © 2023 by Lisa Chamberlain.

All rights reserved. No part of this book may be reproduced in any form without permission in writing from the author. Reviewers may quote brief passages in reviews

Published by **Chamberlain Publications (Wicca Shorts)**

ISBN-13: 978-1-912715-89-3

Disclaimer

No part of this publication may be reproduced or transmitted in any form or by any means, mechanical or electronic, including photocopying or recording, or by any information storage and retrieval system, or transmitted by email without permission in writing from the publisher.

While all attempts have been made to verify the information provided in this publication, neither the author nor the publisher assumes any responsibility for errors, omissions, or contrary interpretations of the subject matter herein.

This book is for entertainment purposes only. The views expressed are those of the author alone, and should not be taken as expert instruction or commands. The reader is responsible for his or her own actions.

Adherence to all applicable laws and regulations, including international, federal, state, and local governing professional licensing, business practices, advertising, and all other aspects of doing business in the US, Canada, or any other jurisdiction is the sole responsibility of the purchaser or reader.

Neither the author nor the publisher assumes any responsibility or liability whatsoever on the behalf of the purchaser or reader of these materials.

Any perceived slight of any individual or organization is purely unintentional.

YOUR FREE GIFT

Thank you for adding this book to your Wiccan library! To learn more, why not join Lisa's Wiccan community and get an exclusive, free spell book?

The book is a great starting point for anyone looking to try their hand at practicing magic. The ten beginner-friendly spells can help you to create a positive atmosphere within your home, protect yourself from negativity, and attract love, health, and prosperity.

Little Book of Spells is now available to read on your laptop, phone, tablet, Kindle or Nook device!

To download, simply visit the following link:

www.wiccaliving.com/bonus

GET THREE FREE AUDIOBOOKS FROM LISA CHAMBERLAIN

Did you know that all of Lisa's books are available in audiobook format? Best of all, you can get **three audiobooks completely free** as part of a 30-day trial with Audible.

Wicca Starter Kit contains three of Lisa's most popular books for beginning Wiccans, all in one convenient place. It's the best and easiest way to learn more about Wicca while also taking audiobooks for a spin! Simply visit:

www.wiccaliving.com/free-wiccan-audiobooks

Alternatively, *Spellbook Starter Kit* is the ideal option for building your magical repertoire using candle and color magic, crystals and mineral stones, and magical herbs. Three spellbooks —over 150 spells—are available in one free volume, here:

www.wiccaliving.com/free-spell-audiobooks

Audible members receive free audiobooks every month, as well as exclusive discounts. It's a great way to experiment and see if audiobook learning works for you.

If you're not satisfied, you can cancel anytime within the trial period. You won't be charged, and you can still keep your books!

CONTENTS

Preface 11

Introduction: Initiations into Self-Care 13

    Why is Self-Care Important? 15
    Integrative Self-Care Practices for Everyday Life 17
    Other Important "Self" Words 21
    Keeping A Self-Care Journal 29
    Setting Up a Self-Care Altar 31
    Working with Deities for Support 33
    Important Note Before Moving Forward 35

Chapter One: **Meditations and Energetic Healing for the Mindful Witch** 36

    Breathing Exercises 37
    White Light Visualization 40
    Magical Cloak Meditation 41
    Meditation Techniques for Clearing the Mind 42
    Body Scan Meditation 45
    Grounding Meditation 47
    Mindful Candle Gazing 49
    Mindful Walk 50
    Meditation Incense Blend 51
    Balancing the Chakras 52
    Chakra Meditation 56

Chapter Two: Crystals for Self-Care: Crystal Healing and Magic 58

Crystal Magic for Well-Being 66
  Crystal Sachet for Grounding Body, Mind, and Spirit 66
  Crystal Sachet to Heal a Broken Heart 67
  Lucky 7 Gratitude Jar to Attract Abundance and Blessings 69
  Crystal Borlw for the Toxic Workplace 70
  Crystals Placed in the Home 72
  Zen Garden for Spiritual Wisdom 73
Crystal Grids 74
  Crystal Grid to Promote Self-Love 75
  Calming Crystal Grid to Promote Peaceful Self-Care 76
  Golden Ratio Spiral Grid for Creative Inspiration 77

Chapter Three: Self-Care for the Kitchen Witch: Magical Foods to Nourish Your Soul 78

Nutritional Magic: Alchemy: Making Positive Changes for Body, Mind, and Spirit 80
Nutritious Foods and Spices and Their Magical Correspondences 83
Preparing Magical Recipes 89
  Good Morning Coffee Spell 91
  Golden Milk Self-Growth Spell 91
  Energy and Detox Sun-Brewed Tea 92
  Rrelaxing Moon-Brewed Tea 93
  Acai Breakfast Bowl for Self-Love 94
  Blissful Tropical Smoothie 95

Buddha Bowl for Abundance.. 96
Chakra Balancing Rainbow Salad............................... 97
Matcha Green Tea Potion for Self-Compassion 99

Chapter Four: Enchanting Self-Care: Aromatherapy, Bath, and Beauty Magic 101

Essential Oilds for Aromatherapeutic and
Magical Uses.. 103
Hands-On Beauty: Magical Self-Care Creations 117
Purifying Face Mask.. 117
Face Serum for Beauty 118
Coffee and Sugar Scrub for Love............................... 119
Peaches and Cream Sweet Talk Lip Scrub................ 120
Bath Salts to Relieve PMS 120
White Light Spray... 121
*Antibacterial Cleaning Spray for Healing
and Purification* 122
Abundance Hand Cream... 123
Earthing Foot Scrub 124
Soothing Milk and Honey Bath................................... 125
Essential Oil Blends for Magical Self-Care.................... 127
Tension and Headache Oil Blend............................... 128
Deep Breath Oil Blend 129
Heart Healing Oil Blend.. 130
Wise Student Oil Blend... 131
Friendship Oil Blend.. 132
Spiritual Awakening Oil Blend..................................... 133

Chapter Five: Botanical Magic: Self-Care for the Green Witch 134

Gardens for Self-Care 148

Indoor Plant Power 150
Self-Care Spellcrafts for the Green Witch 152
   Loose Leaf Incense for Courage 152
   Solar Success Loose Leaf Incense 153
   Loose Leaf Incense for Psychic Visions 154
   Spell Bottle to Ease Depression 155
   Spell Bottle for the Highly Sensitive Person 156
   Peace and Love Bath Tea 157
   Sweet Dreams Sleeping Sachet 158
   Magical Sachet for Self-Esteem 159
   Get Well Soon Healing Sachet 160
   Protective Boundary Powder 161

Chapter Six: Intuitive Self-Care: Divination and Other Tools to Deepen Your Practice 162

Working with a Pendulum 164
Intuition Exercise: Green Light/Red Light 167
Working with Your Dreams 169
Personal Development in the Tarot Court Cards 172
Card Spread for Self-Care 183
   Simple Check-In Spread 183
   Comforting Card Spread 184
   Self-Awareness Spread 185

Conclusion 187

   Suggestions for Further Reading 188
   About the Authors 190

PREFACE

The word "self-care" seems to mean different things to different people. Some may picture a massage session or a night out with friends, while others may think about exercise routines and regular dental visits. Self-care can be all of these things, and much more.

Many people are aware of the importance of self-care to long-term well-being, but still treat it as a special occasion—something that we try to fit into our schedules once in a while, rather than making it central to our way of life. For others, self-care may even have an air of frivolousness about it—a luxury we can't afford when we already have so much going on in our days.

For many years, I was in that second group. Against the backdrop of all my daily responsibilities, which I already believed there wasn't enough time for, the idea of self-care seemed like a waste of time. What did my own well-being matter when there were classes to teach, papers to grade, and dinner to get on the table? What I didn't know then is that if I had just taken some time for myself, my experience of time would have expanded, and all the other details would have fallen into place with much less effort and anxiety.

Fortunately, I have finally learned that lesson, and the privilege of working on this collaboration with Kiki Dombrowski, my co-author, has helped me anchor it even more firmly into my approach to life. There are many books about self-care these days, but this one is tailored for witches, which is, of course, right up my alley. In the course of the editing process, I discovered new crystals and oils to work with, new ways of connecting with my intuition, and even a new framework for working with the Tarot for personal development.

Kiki is a well-known writer on all things divination, as well as other topics in witchcraft and magic. A frequent guest on numerous magic and witchcraft-related podcasts, she is also a teacher and life coach, and her wisdom shines through in these pages. The vision for this book, and most of the content, comes from Kiki's creative take on magical self-care. I edited the initial draft and have added my thoughts to the chapter overviews, as well as many details throughout the book.

Like magic itself, self-care is a life-long journey. It's a continual process that benefits us for as long as we're here on Earth. And, just like the study of magic, we can't do it all at once. We try new things, give them time, and learn from our results. You may find success with some of the approaches in this book, and no discernible change with others. You may have an initial burst of enthusiasm for starting new daily habits, like a meditation routine, and wind up dropping it by the fourth day.

This is common, and not a sign that you're doing it "wrong." True progress is rarely linear. It's much more like a dance—moving forwards, backwards, and in circles. But before long, you will notice (as I finally did) that life gets so much better—and more magical— when you take the time to do what works best for you, whenever you can.

I invite you to take this journey one step at a time. Explore what inspires you, experiment with a wide variety of practices, and observe the magical transformations you experience along your path of self-care.

— **Lisa Chamberlain, Editor and Co-author**

INTRODUCTION: INITIATIONS INTO SELF-CARE

The topic of self-care is enjoying increasing popularity at the moment—and that is to the benefit of everyone.

Originating in the medical world in the mid-20th century, and ultimately becoming something of a beauty industry "buzzword" over the past several years, self-care is a term used to describe making the prioritized effort to take care of yourself. It involves taking mindful and positive actions and developing healthy habits in your life to improve your well-being, mood, and livelihood.

Engaging consciously in self-care allows you experience relief, comfort, health, and personal growth. It also offers the opportunity for spiritual development. Until recently, self-care has not been much of a focus in books and discussions around witchcraft, but happily, the tide is changing.

If you're reading this book, you have already shown that you are interested in taking time to care for yourself and incorporate practices into your life that allow you to feel more balance, wellness, abundance, peace, and joy. You're also likely looking for ways to improve your well-being that are fun, creative, and magical, and not merely more "tasks" to add to your to-do list.

This book provides a wide range of hands-on, magical self-care tools and practices that will inspire you in new ways to take care of the most important person in your life—*you*. We'll cover meditation and mindfulness practices, crystals for healing and magical grid work, holistic kitchen witchery, aromatherapeutic and herbal spell crafts, and divination and intuitive practices for enhancing spiritual well-being.

But first, let's take a deeper dive into the broader context of self-care. What does self-care look like, in practice? What are the benefits of developing regular self-care? Beyond the basics of looking after our bodies, what else does self-care entail? How can we integrate self-care into our magical practice, and magic into our self-care practice? The following discussions will address these questions and more.

WHY IS SELF-CARE IMPORTANT?

"Nourishing yourself in a way that helps you blossom in the direction you want to go is attainable, and you are worth the effort." — **Deborah Day**

Self-care is especially important for witches and magical people, who tend to be empaths and highly sensitive. It is important for them to have self-care practices in place so they do not feel drained, burned out, or burdened by other people's issues.

- Self-care helps you respond more skillfully to challenging situations.
- Self-care helps you feel more inspired and energized.
- Self-care allows you to listen to yourself more effectively.
- Self-care can you lead to discovering new talents and opportunities.
- Self-care makes you excited about and aware of your own improvements and accomplishments.
- Self-care assists you in developing a healthy relationship with yourself.
- Self-care facilitates more effective magic by strengthening your personal power.

Through self-care, we feel better about ourselves and situations, giving ourselves the opportunity to feel peace and hope. Taking care of yourself in the present moment means you are establishing practices that will help you cultivate success, health, and wellness for your future.

INTEGRATIVE SELF-CARE PRACTICES FOR EVERYDAY LIFE

"Self-care means being switched on, fully present and engaged in your life. It's the opposite of switching off and retreating from the world. Ignoring your own needs leaves you depleted, but self-care will energize and recharge you."
— **Nadia Narain and Katia Narain Philips**

While this book will focus on magical self-care tools and practices, it's important to remember that overall wellness is built on a foundation of daily habits and regular activities that work together to allow our bodies and minds to function optimally.

You will find so much improvement in every aspect of your experience by consciously integrating these practices into your way of life, whether or not you ever work any magic. That said, the bonus benefit for witches is that these practices will boost the magical outcomes of the self-care activities throughout this book. Keep the following suggestions in mind to help you stay on track in the "mundane" world as you explore the magical side of self-care.

- **Eating Well & Staying Hydrated:** Follow a healthy diet full of greens and superfoods, and avoid eating too many processed foods. Remember to stay hydrated and drink at least 8 glasses of purified water each day.
- **Healthy Sleeping Habits:** Each person is different, but on average adults need to sleep between 7 and 9 hours a night. Try to keep electronic devices away from the bed—if you use your phone as an alarm, keep it in airplane mode at night. Make your bedroom as comfortable, cool, and quiet as possible.
- **Personal Hygiene:** Keeping up with personal hygiene makes you feel good, and is a simple practice you can be proud to accomplish, especially if you are feeling depressed. Daily hygiene practices include brushing and flossing your teeth, showering, brushing your hair, putting on fresh clothes, washing your hands, and keeping your nails clean.
- **Mental Health Care:** Fortunately, seeing a therapist is widely accepted as a healthy practice these days—there is no need to feel embarrassed about seeing someone to help with our mental health. A licensed counselor can help you develop mental wellness through psychological practices such as cognitive behavioral therapy, dialectical behavior therapy, or even EMDR treatment. You may also want to consider visiting with a licensed life coach to help hold you accountable for goals and practices.
- **Personal Time:** Having time alone is necessary to recuperate, rest, and restore the mind and body. Solitude is also valuable for learning how to be more aware of your feelings and become more familiar with yourself.

- **Social Time:** For the vast majority of us, it's also important to feel we are part of a community. Having a trusting and loving support system of people you like to spend time with can bring excitement and change into your regular routine. Witches may want to consider finding a reputable coven to join, or magical classes to participate in. There are also plenty of metaphysical retreats and Pagan gatherings where you can connect with like-minded souls.
- **Comforting Activities:** Take a moment to pause right now. Ask yourself: when is the last time I felt super comfortable? Once you can recall this moment, lean into the memory of how you felt. Hold onto this feeling and build on it in your present moment. What can you do in the near future to experience this feeling again? Find ways to bring comforting rituals and routines into your life to ease stress and anxiety.
- **Physical Activity & Exercise:** Getting your body to move and stretch helps to maintain your physical wellness. It's also ideal to work up a light sweat at least once a day, if possible. There are so many different ways to get your body moving that you could try a different one every day for a month until you find the ones that best suit you! Popular physical activities include daily walks, stretching, yoga, Pilates, running, swimming, and so on, but you can also get exercise by mowing the lawn or mopping the floor. Don't set yourself up to fail by overcommitting, though. If you can exercise three times per week, great. If you have to start with one time per week, great. Gradual change is the best way to make lasting change.
- **Professional Empowerment:** We may not like our day jobs, but they may provide security and money for us

that we need to survive comfortably. We can all continue to empower ourselves professionally by taking workshops to improve our skills, updating our resume, and networking with and shadowing those in the career fields we hope to achieve. Keeping your focus on where you want to go, rather than on feeling stuck or trapped where you are, is key to maintaining mental and emotional health, as well as to manifesting your professional goals.

- **Financial Balance:** Finding financial balance in the modern-day world is a struggle for many. Simply having enough to have a saving account can feel like a privilege. But the more we face our financial struggles, ask for help, maintain paying our bills, and work to improve our financial income, the more secure we will feel. While this book will offer spells and spell ingredients for money and abundance, sometimes the best magic we conjure for prosperity is through a good knowledge of budgeting skills and knowing how to spend wisely. We also benefit by appreciating what we have, which generates the energetic frequency of abundance and an overall feeling of well-being.

- **Giving Back:** In their final song recorded as a quartet, the Beatles sang to the world a profound incantation: "The love you take is equal to the love you make." There is so much magical value in giving love, compassion, support, and charity to those in need. You will find that if you can give back, volunteer, or simply be an active listener to a companion, you will feel more connected and full of love.

OTHER IMPORTANT "SELF" WORDS

Self-care can be an be an umbrella term that encompasses many other related "self" words.

The 13 words below represent different (but often related) aspects of self-care. Our lives are built from our daily actions, attitudes, beliefs, and thought patterns, many of which are unconscious. Reflecting on the concepts below can help you identify positive activities, practices, and exercises to enhance your quality of life, and ways to help release habits or patterns of thought that aren't serving you.

Here you will find inspirational quotes from thought leaders in the self-care realm, affirmations to work with to embody the concepts, and suggestions for incorporating the energies of these important components of self-care into your daily life.

SELF-MAINTENANCE

"Our bodies are our gardens, to which our wills are gardeners." — **William Shakespeare**

Self-maintenance is the act of taking care of yourself, often in regard to your personal hygiene and habits. This could include grooming habits, eating habits, and sleeping habits.

An affirmation to focus your intention on self-maintenance would be *"I maintain myself to remain balanced and healthy."* To work more with self-maintenance, review the list of integrative self-care practices in the introduction (above), read about nourishing and magical foods in Chapter 3, and try the bath products in Chapter 4.

SELF-DISCIPLINE

"Self-discipline is caring." — **M. Scott Peck**

Self-discipline is the act of pursuing positive motivation and developing the willpower to refrain from acting in a way that would be harmful. Self-discipline is a way of regulating the way you behave or think so that you live a healthier and safer life. This may even include building boundaries to protect yourself from psychic depletion or being taken advantage of, or budgeting time and balancing responsibilities to avoid burnout.

An affirmation to focus your intention on self-discipline would be *"I have the discipline to do what is best for me because what I do now prepares me for the best future."* To work more with self-discipline, try creating the Focus Oil blend in Chapter 4 and wear it when you need to concentrate or stay on task with a project.

SELF-FORGIVENESS

"Choose, every day, to forgive yourself. You are human, flawed, and most of all worthy of love." — **Alison Malee**

Self-forgiveness is the act of releasing anger or resentment toward yourself. While examining how we behave and react in situations is an important part of reflection and growth, being excessively critical or cruel to ourselves in the process is not helpful, but is actually harmful. Self-forgiveness is being aware when you feel unnecessary guilt or shame about a situation and forgiving yourself for those feelings.

An affirmation to focus your intention on self-forgiveness would be *"I am growing and evolving. I forgive myself, knowing I made the best choices I could during the situation I was facing."* To work more with self-forgiveness, try using the Healing Heart Oil in Chapter 4.

SELF-ESTEEM

"To establish true self-esteem, we must concentrate on our successes and forget about the failures and the negatives in our lives." — **Denis Waitley**

Self-esteem is the way you feel about yourself. It is how you value yourself and represents the conscious and unconscious feelings you have about yourself, for better or worse. Self-esteem is something we all working on improving!

An affirmation to focus your intention on self-esteem would be *"I hold myself in high esteem because I am valuable, lovable, unique, and magical."* To work more with self-esteem, drink the Blissful Tropical Smoothie in Chapter 3 and carry the Self-Esteem Sachet from Chapter 5.

SELF-DEVELOPMENT

"Invent your world. Surround yourself with people, color, sounds, and work that will nourish you." — **Susan Ariel Rainbow Kennedy (SARK)**

Self-development is the act of developing personal skills, abilities, talents, hobbies, and interests that enrich your life and allow you to discover more about who you are and what you love to do.

An affirmation to focus your intention on self-development would be *"I develop my skills, talents, and magic to be a masterful spirit of this universe."* To work more with self-development, identify the topics and discussions in this book that light you up and focus on those areas first. Create goals for yourself, write them down in your journal (see "Journaling Your Needs," below), and honor yourself for the progress you've made. You can also study the personality archetypes of the Tarot court cards in Chapter 6, and try the Golden Milk for Self-Growth spell in Chapter 3.

SELF-LOVE

"To love oneself is the beginning of a lifelong romance." — **Oscar Wilde**

Self-love is the ability to love yourself holistically and afford yourself the same treatment and care that you would for anyone you deeply love and admire. It is taking time to celebrate who you are and appreciate what you are doing.

An affirmation to focus your intention on self-love would be *"I love myself because I am a reflection of a magical world and a divine creator."* To work more with self-love, use the Self-Love Crystal Grid in Chapter 2 while enjoying the Acai Breakfast Bowl for Self-Love in Chapter 3.

SELF-COMPASSION

"When we give ourselves compassion, we are opening our hearts in ways that can transform lives." — **Kristin Neff**

Self-compassion is the quality of being patient, tender, and kind to yourself. It is giving yourself the opportunity to be understanding with the way you've felt as you walk through obstacles.

An affirmation to focus your intention on self-compassion would be *"I am deserving of compassion, and I offer myself the same tenderness and comfort I give to others."* To work more with self-compassion, read about green calcite in Chapter 2 and drink Matcha Green Tea Potion from Chapter 3.

SELF-EXPRESSION

"I am my own muse. I am the subject I know best. The subject I want to know better." — **Frida Kahlo**

Self-expression is the act of expressing your feelings and thoughts in a way that helps you better perceive yourself and what you are experiencing. It is a way of being vulnerable with yourself and the world around you, which allows you to reveal your needs, desires, hopes, and fears.

An affirmation to focus your intention on self-expression would be *"My voice and observations matter. My expression is creative, hopeful, and inspiring."* To work more with self-expression, get inspired by "Gardens for Self-Care" in Chapter 5 and work more intentionally with your dreams as discussed in Chapter 6. Also consider journaling, writing a blog, creating visual artwork, speaking with a friend, or talking to a licensed therapist to get your thoughts and feelings out.

SELF-TALK

"Talk to yourself like you would to someone you love." — **Brene Brown**

Self-talk is the experience of talking to yourself in your mind—it is the inner dialogue you personally hear internally. Self-talk may guide you to make certain decisions, or respond or feel a certain way in any given situation, and the quality of these responses will be related to the quality of your self-talk. Monitoring how we talk to ourselves can help us deflate a tense situation, identify when we need to pause and re-center, and shift our mood to a more peaceful place.

An affirmation to focus your intention on healthier self-talk would be *"I speak kindly to myself and patiently observe and release patterns of negative self-talk.* To work more with self-talk, try to be more cognizant when you say something negative to yourself, and counteract it by saying three positive things. Also, try using the Peaches and Cream Sweet Talk Lip Scrub in Chapter 3.

SELF-DISCOVERY

"You will recognize your own path when you come upon it, because you will suddenly have all the energy and imagination you ever need." — **Jerry Gillies**

Self-discovery is the act of discovering something new and special about yourself. This can be an inspirational breakthrough, a great idea that will help you prosper, or a moment when you realize something profoundly true about yourself.

An affirmation to focus your intention on self-discovery would be *"I am discovering what makes me feel the best, what inspires me, and what helps me manifest success."* To work more with self-discovery, try the Body Scan Meditation in Chapter 1, explore the personality archetypes of the Tarot court cards in Chapter 6, and try the Self-Care divination spreads in Chapter 6.

SELF-SEEKING

"It is so important to take time for yourself and find clarity. The most important relationship is the one you have with yourself." — **Diane Von Furstenburg**

Self-seeking is the act of pursuing a deeper understanding of who you are and what makes you tick. It is a proactive endeavor that helps you discover answers to questions you may have about yourself, your soul path, and perhaps even what your place is in this universe.

An affirmation to focus your intention on self-seeking pursuits would be *"I am seeking higher knowledge, wisdom, and truth to give my life purpose and direction."* To work more with self-seeking pursuits, build the Golden Ratio Spiral Grid in Chapter 2 and wear the Wise Student Oil in chapter 4.

SELF-AWARENESS

"To be yourself in a world that is constantly trying to make you something else is the greatest accomplishment." — **Ralph Waldo Emerson**

Self-awareness is the ability to deeply know who you are and your place in the cosmos. It is a sense of being rooted in yourself—the ability to identify what you are feeling physically, emotionally, and spiritually.

An affirmation to focus your intention on self-awareness would be *"I am aware of my inner and outer worlds and find pleasure in seeing them harmoniously interact with each other."* To work more with self-awareness, try using the Spiritual Awakening Oil in Chapter 4, burning the Loose Leaf Incense for Psychic Visions in Chapter 5, and using the Self-Awareness Spread in Chapter 6.

SELF-GRATITUDE

"Acknowledging the good that you have in your life is the foundation for all abundance." — **Eckhart Tolle**

Self-gratitude is the act of feeling gratitude for your own abilities, uniqueness, growth and opportunities. It is being thankful for your wellness, abundances, experiences, relationships, and lessons.

An affirmation to focus your intention on self-gratitude would be *"I am grateful for the opportunity to take care of myself, and grateful for all that I have experienced in this lifetime."* To work more with self-gratitude, take a few minutes every night before bed to think, talk, or write about three things you were thankful for that day, and create the Gratitude Jar in Chapter 2.

KEEPING A SELF-CARE JOURNAL

As mentioned in the Preface to this book, self-care is a continual process and a life-long journey. Recording your experience of this journey at regular intervals is an excellent way to anchor new practices more solidly into your daily life, and to expand your awareness of the changes taking place in your physical, emotional, and spiritual experience. Interestingly, the words "journal" and "journey" both come from the same Latin root word (*diurnalis*).

Whether you are comfortable with keeping a traditional journal, or prefer to just jot down daily notes on your feelings and activities, I recommend having a designated place to record your experiences as you move along through this book. Identify the ideas, workings, recipes and practices you feel most inspired to try, and make note afterwards of which ones resonate most with your individual needs and desires. What has been effective and enjoyable? What hasn't brought the results you were looking for? What new desires are these practices inspiring in you?

The following writing prompts can help you uncover what is most valuable to you on your unique self-care journey.

- What does self-care mean to you?
- What areas in your life are you hoping to see improvement in?

- How do you think it would feel to experience these improvements?
- What was it that inspired you to read this book?
- What integrative self-care practices (from the discussion above) would you most benefit from focusing on at this time?
- What role do you think magic might play for you when it comes to self-care?
- List three things that make you feel magical.
- How do you like to express your magical abilities?
- Give yourself three compliments.
- Write about a time you felt in balance and at peace.

SETTING UP A SELF-CARE ALTAR

While it could be argued that all altars foster a space for self-care, the following recommendations can help you create an intentional space that focuses specifically on your own self-care needs and interests.

If you already keep a permanent altar, consider transforming and re-dedicating it for this purpose, at least while you work with this book. Or, depending on your available space, you can create an additional altar with a self-care focus.

If you don't have a permanent altar, try dedicating a shelf or other surface that enables you to create one for this purpose. As your self-care practice deepens, you may find yourself wanting to update the items on your altar to reflect where you are currently on your journey.

- **Living plants:** Plants are amazing for transforming an atmosphere. There is a list of recommended magical indoor plants in Chapter 5. You may also want to dress your altar with vibrant and beautiful flowers. Fresh bouquets are a wonderful addition—especially daisies, orchids, and roses.

- **Crystals:** Healing crystals that work wonderfully for those on a self-care journey include lepidolite, rhodochrosite, green calcite, rose quartz, howlite, and unakite. Be sure to investigate the crystals featured in

Chapter 2 for any additional crystals that may speak to you personally at this time.

- **Magical tools, amulets, and talismans:** Personalizing your self-care altar with trinkets from places you've visited, talismans for good luck and protection, or magical tools such as an athame or cauldron, will raise the magical energy of the space.

- **Pictures of ancestors, gods, or goddesses:** If you feel a connection with one or more of your ancestors, or feel called to work with any deities, you can represent them on your altar. You will find a list of deities from various cultures that you may wish to work with in the next section, below.

- **Artistic creations:** If you are artistic, you may want to include a favorite personal project, or create something new that represents your current dreams and desires for well-being.

- **Vision board:** A vision board is a collage of pictures and words that are meant to help you feel motivated and inspired about manifesting dreams. You can dream big: incorporate images and affirmations that represent the best results you can imagine.

- **Journals or books on self-care:** The act of placing a book on your altar demonstrates your commitment to pursuing the topic of the book in earnest. The Selected Bibliography at the end of this book will give you some ideas for books to start with.

WORKING WITH DEITIES FOR SUPPORT

If your practice incorporates work with deities from ancient and/or existing pagan cultures, this diverse list may point you to sources of divine support. Even if you don't feel called to establish a relationship with deities, studying the myths of any that interest you may inspire new ideas or directions to move toward along your self-care journey.

- **If you need emotional support and nurturing:** Demeter, Gaia, Great Mother, Green Tara, Hestia, Isis, Kuan-Yin, Lakshmi, Ninsun, White Buffalo Calf Woman

- **If you are going through a transformative or transitory time:** Baba Yaga, Epione, Ganesh, Hecate, Janus, Kuan Yin, La'amaomao, Osiris, Rhiannon, Yemaya

- **For developing your intellect and sharpening innate skills:** Athena, Eir, Hermes, Lugh, Minerva, Seshat, Thoth

- **For improving physical health and fostering healing in your life:** Aja, Apollo, Asclepius, Brahma, Brigid, Dhanvantari, Eir, Itzamna, Ix Chel, Osanyin, Sekhmet

- **For bringing more happiness and fun into your life:** Bast, Belun, Brahma, Cernunnos, Cocomama,

Euphrosyne, Fu Shen, Krishna, Koros, Laetitia, Lilith, Pan, Shiva, Wopeh

- **If you are deepening your spirituality:** Bast, Dagda, Freyja, Hecate, Hermes, Isis, Odin, Psyche, Selene, Tara, Vishnu
- **If you are building up your self-esteem, self-love, and sense of self-worth:** Aphrodite, Freyja, Gwen, Lilith, Inanna, Krishna, Ohsun, Pavarti, Venus
- **For finding your inner warrior and feeling empowered:** Artemis, Atalanta, Diana, Durga, Horus, Odin, Tyr
- **If you wish to feel inspired and artistic:** Arachne, Brigid, Ceridwen, Ix Chel, Saraswati
- **For learning about boundaries and how to protect yourself from harm:** Acaia, Angak, Bes, Green Tara, Pele
- **For building your career and bringing more prosperity into your life:** Abundantia, Aje, Anuket, Chicomecoatl, Dagda, Ganesh, Lakshmi, Maeve
- **If you want more adventure in your life and are ready to explore the world:** Mercury, Rhiannon

IMPORTANT NOTE BEFORE MOVING FORWARD

When reviewing the herbs, oils, foods, and activities suggested in this book, please keep in mind any physical limitations or special health conditions you may have. In other words: if you are very sensitive to essential oils, please be mindful in using them on your skin.

If you have many food allergies, speak to your doctor or nutritionist before incorporating new herbs and foods into your diet. If you have had depression or anxiety for longer than two weeks, speak to a professional therapist who is clinically trained to help you emerge from feeling badly. Do what you can, take your time, and be tender and patient with yourself.

Chapter One: MEDITATIONS AND ENERGETIC HEALING FOR THE MINDFUL WITCH

One of the most powerful tools of self-care is mindfulness. Mindfulness is being aware of your present moment. When you are being mindful, you are engaged with what is happening around you through your five senses, rather than or the past—which is where our thoughts are often focused.

Practices such as yoga and qi gong are known for their ability to facilitate a mindful state of awareness, using physical motions and postures that allow you to feel energy moving through your body in the present moment. Meditation is an excellent way to help quiet the mind, as you direct your attention inwards, releasing thoughts associated with stress, worry, fear, resentment, anger, etc. Being mindful can make you feel a greater sense of peace and comfort, which allows you to make better decisions and navigate life's ups and downs with greater ease.

This chapter will guide you through different meditations and physical activities that will help you to be more mindful.

BREATHING EXERCISES

We breathe, on average, about 23,000 times a day. Yet we can take for granted how very precious each breath can be to our wellness. If we focus on our breath throughout the day, we can help keep ourselves grounded, centered, and open to inspiration and guidance from the spirit world.

Here are some ways to use the simple tool of the breath for improving your overall well-being. Try each exercise and make a practice of the one(s) that you feel the most benefit from.

- Spend a few moments breathing in and out through your nose only. Keep your mouth closed with your molars touching and tongue resting on the roof of your mouth. Notice any sensations in your heart chakra area. This type of breath helps to awaken the body.
- The following 4:7:8 breath practice was created by Dr. Andrew Weil. Sit with your legs crossed and back straight, with your shoulders back and your chin poised. If you cannot sit with your legs crossed, you can also sit up straight on a chair with your back flat against the back of the chair. Keep a steady count in your head, breathing in for a count of 4, holding your breath for a count of 7, and breathing out of your

mouth for a count of 8. Notice any changes in how you feel.

- Diaphragmatic breathing techniques are meant to help you feel breath deep in your belly. Lie down so your body is flat, but comfortable. Take a deep and gentle breath in through your nose, until you feel your belly fill up completely. Slowly and gently exhale through your mouth, taking twice as long to breathe out as you did to breathe in. If you have asthma or sleep apnea, you may want to breathe out of your mouth through pursed lips, as if you were going to whistle.

- *Nadi Shodhana* is a yoga technique also known as "Alternative Nostril Breathing." For this exercise, sit cross-legged or sit straight up in a chair with your back tall, chin poised, and hands softly resting on your thighs. You may want to check to make sure that your tongue is resting on the roof of your mouth, with your molars touching and lips resting shut, to ensure your mouth is completely closed. Close your eyes and roll your shoulders. You can also stretch your neck a little by gently tilting your neck towards your left shoulder, slowly rolling your head down towards your chest, and then tilting your neck towards your right shoulder, before returning upwards. This exercise may seem complicated at first glance, but in practice it flows very easily once you get the hang of it:

    1. Take your right hand and fold your index finger and middle finger into your palm.
    2. Now, with your right hand in position to do the exercise, seal your right nostril with your thumb.

3. Inhale through your left nostril.
4. Hold your breath and remove your thumb from your right nostril.
5. With your ring finger, seal your left nostril.
6. Exhale through your right nostril.
7. With your ring finger still sealing your left nostril, inhale through your right nostril.
8. Hold your breath and remove your ring finger from your left nostril.
9. Once again, seal your right nostril with your thumb.
10. Exhale through the left nostril.
11. Repeat this cycle five to ten times. It can be an excellent morning practice before starting the day!

WHITE LIGHT VISUALIZATION

This simple visualization is one that many magical practitioners and metaphysicians love. It is believed that, by visualizing white light surrounding your body, you can protect your auric field from negativity and dark influences. Many like to use this visualization while doing magical or psychic work, but you can also use it any time you are feeling exposed or intuitively uncomfortable.

Close your eyes and take deep, slow breaths. Using your mind's eye, visualize a bright, powerful circle of white light surrounding you. Some people envision this as a solid light glowing brightly, others see it as glittering white star dust, and still others see it as a shining crystal. Perhaps you see all of those forms, or something different! Envision this white light all around you—see it surrounding you in a shell of protective and loving energy, knowing that it will guard you from harm.

MAGICAL CLOAK MEDITATION

If you are looking for a more magical interpretation of the White Light Visualization, you can also try visualizing a magical cloak. Close your eyes and take deep, slow breaths. Using your mind's eye, visualize yourself holding a magical cloak. This cloak represents your personal magic and power. It can be velvet or satin, linen or silk—whatever you love the most. The outside layer is a deep purple or indigo color and reminds you of the night sky. Perhaps you even see spirals or the moon embroidered into the fabric. The inside layer is white with golden threads running through it.

Wrap the cloak over your shoulders, feeling its warmth and heaviness. As the fabric surrounds you, you begin to feel energized with magical energy, feeling inner wisdom, intuition, and the ability to perform sacred witchcraft.

MEDITATION TECHNIQUES FOR CLEARING THE MIND

You will often hear it said that you have to have a clear mind during meditation. However, if you have an active and thoughtful mind full of wonderful ideas and a vibrant imagination, it can sound like an impossible feat to "clear" your mind.

In actuality, clearing your mind is simply a means of disengaging with the whirlwind of thoughts running through your mind, many of which can be critical and anxious. Meditation helps purify the mind by pulling you into the present moment.

Here are some techniques that can help you experience a clear, restful mind in the present moment:

- Make meditation a routine ritual. Designate a quiet area where you won't be disturbed, and create an atmosphere conducive to meditation: use a specific oil blend for the purpose in your diffuser, light a candle, and/or bring a calming crystal or two. Begin to schedule your meditation practice at the same time every day.

- As you sit in meditation, any time a thought comes through your mind, treat it like a passing cloud. Envision it moving by and quieting as it passes.
- If a thought comes into your mind, push it away when you breathe out, letting it blow out of your active mind.
- Try and listen to the sounds furthest away from you. This might actually be "brown noise," or a hum that is generated by the sounds of the environment around you.
- Visualize the thought in your mind turning and blowing away like dust or sand, being erased, or being washed away with clean water.
- Visualize shapes. You may want to experiment with visualizing shapes being drawn from your breath, such as a spiral, an infinity sign, a pyramid, or even sacred flower shapes.
- Listen to binaural beats or other calming sounds on headphones.
- Tell yourself a simple mantra when you have thoughts coming in. Simply repeating the mantra "Om" (pronounced "aummm") in your mind, or aloud, may help to let them flow away.
- Focus on your breath—on how it sounds, and how it feels moving through your nose, into your lungs, pressed out of your lungs, and out of your nose.
- Be okay with thoughts coming in. They will not spoil your mediation. In your mind, thank them and do not brood on them.

<u>Note</u>: don't worry if your meditation session feels like a struggle to get to that "clear state." Just making the effort for 10-15 minutes per day will bring results. Often, the

benefits of meditating aren't felt during the meditation, but afterwards—sometimes hours later. If you establish a consistent practice, you will notice more ease in your mind after a few days, and you will find it easier to achieve a clear state over time.

BODY SCAN MEDITATION

A body scan meditation is a powerful way to engage with your body, remain in the present moment, and relieve stress and tension. This meditation can be done sitting upright or lying down. I think it feels especially comfortable to try while lying down in the grass under the sun.

Close your eyes and take long, slow, deep breaths, feeling the breath fill deep into your belly. Feel the weight of your body on the chair or ground, noticing the sensation of your weight pressing down. You will then start scanning your body, starting at your feet and moving upwards.

First focus on your feet, noticing any sensations in them. Perhaps there is a tingling feeling. Are they itchy? Are they hot or cold? They may just feel neutral—if so, just notice how they interact with their environment.

Notice the sensations in your feet and identify whether you are holding any tension there. If so, loosen or relax your muscles to give them relief, softening any holding or stress. If your feet are an area where you feel illness or discomfort, you are invited to envision them surrounded by green, blue, and white light, glowing with healing relief.

Next, move upwards to your calves. Again, notice any sensations in this area. Perhaps your calves feel tight or tense, itchy or tingly. You may notice if they feel hot, cold, or neutral.

Again, identify whether you are holding any tension. If so, loosen or relax the muscles in your calves to give them relief, softening any holding or stress there. If your calves are an area where you feel illness or discomfort, you are invited to envision the area surrounded by green, blue, and white light, glowing with healing relief.

Continue scanning upwards, repeating the process above. Places to stop include your knees, thighs, groin region, intestines and lower abdomen, under the rib cage, lungs, throat and neck, shoulders, arms, hands, temples, and head.

GROUNDING MEDITATION

You will hear many folks in magical and metaphysical communities talk about the importance of grounding. Grounding is a means of reconnecting with earth energy. This is an especially important practice for those who do spiritual work, feel scattered, or need to feel more stable and centered.

Below is a meditative visualization to help you feel anchored and connected with earth. You can do this meditation standing up or sitting down. You can also do this lying down, with your knees bent and feet flat on the ground.

It is especially powerful to do this meditation outside with bare feet touching the grass, soil, or sand—this is known as "earthing," as it allows the body to connect with the natural electric charge of the earth. Keep your feet flat on the ground, directly under your hips (if standing), with a strong and straight posture. I once heard a yoga teacher say that you should have your chest raised to share your heart with divine source—perhaps this will inspire you to maintain a good posture.

Close your eyes, turning your attention to your breath. Deepen and slow your breath. Focus on your feet touching the earth. How does the ground feel underneath you?

Recognize its stable and strong hold, supporting you and connecting you to the earth.

    Visualize roots growing from the bottom of your feet, or from the base of your spine. Envision these roots growing deeper and deeper into the earth. As they grow, feel how anchored you are to the earth, trusting that you are stable and secure. You may feel like you are magnetically connected to the earth, or feel a heavy but comforting weight on you, making you ever aware of how solidly your feet are planted in the ground. Take a moment to feel these roots connect throughout your body, taking a few extra deep breaths before opening your eyes.

MINDFUL CANDLE GAZING

Think about the last time you sat in front of a fire and admired the flames moving and changing. Watching a fire can be a hypnotic experience that allows you to gently focus your attention on its warm and empowering energy.

For this simple meditation, you will need only a candle. Set the candle up so there is blank wall behind it. Light the candle and turn off the lights in the room. Stare intently into the candle. If you like, you can let your focus go soft as you watch the flame move. Any time you feel your attention slipping, go back to deeply watching the flame.

Some people will even use candles as an opportunity to scry, which is the art of gazing to reveal divinatory messages. As you gaze into the candle, see if any shapes take form that gently impart a message to you.

MINDFUL WALK

Any activity, in theory, can be mindful. However, mindful walks are gratifying because you can observe many things, walk in a space of mental peace, and also get your body doing a little physical activity.

Next time you take a walk, slow down your pace, put your phone away in your pocket (or even better, leave it at home), and start to observe everything around you. Focus on your feet touching the ground. Feel them press against the ground, the heels, soles, and toes coming in contact with the earth and then pushing up. Notice the rhythm of your breath as you move, trying to keep it steady and comfortable.

Witches have the added bonus of taking in the surroundings in a magical way. Do you notice any animals? Do any images appear in the clouds in front of you? What does it feel like to be supported by Mother Earth? Take the opportunity to observe magic in every step of your mindful walk.

MEDITATION INCENSE BLEND

This is a simple blend of resins that you can mix together and burn on a charcoal briquette in a fire-safe container. You only need a small pinch—resins can make a lot of aromatic smoke!

You will need:

- 2 parts Frankincense
- 2 parts Myrrh
- 2 parts Copal
- 1 part Benzoin

Instructions:

Crush the resins with a mortar and pestle. Keep in mind that this will take a little elbow grease—both to crush as well as to clean the mortar afterwards. However, smaller pieces of the resins are easier to work with.

Once the resins are ground to smaller pieces and well blended, you may add in a couple drops of lotus and sandalwood essential oils.

BALANCING THE CHAKRAS

Chakras are energy points within our bodies. The word *chakra* comes from the Sanskrit word meaning "wheel," and the chakras are said to be spinning spirals (or vortices) of energy moving in and around the body.

There are seven major chakras running up the center of the body, from the base of the spine to the top of our head, and each rules over specific functions.

ROOT CHAKRA

- **Location:** Base of the spine
- **Associations:** Survival, determination, "fight or flight" response, security, practicalities
- **Signs of Balance:** Feeling safe and secure, feeling accomplished, connection to family and earth
- **Signs of Imbalance:** Phobias, feeling stuck or trapped, isolation, anxiety
- **How to balance, heal, treat:** Try reflexology, wear or visualize red, use patchouli or vetiver oils, practice the yogic crow pose or mountain pose, hold garnet or fire agate, eat root vegetables

SACRAL CHAKRA

- **Location:** Sacrum, in the pelvic bowl near the sex organs
- **Associations:** Sexuality, desire, pleasure, stamina, confidence
- **Signs of Balance:** Feeling warmth, healthy sexual function, fun-loving, and outgoing
- **Signs of Imbalance:** Urinary problems, menstrual issues, lethargy, lower back issues
- **How to balance, heal, treat:** Try a hot salt bath, wear or visualize orange, use ylang ylang or rosewood oils, practice yogic pelvic lifts, hold carnelian or tangerine quartz, eat oranges or mangoes

SOLAR PLEXUS CHAKRA

- **Location:** Below breastbone, navel region
- **Associations:** Creativity, self-esteem, transformation, respect, center of the "gut feeling"
- **Signs of Balance:** Feeling creative, brave, empowered, assertive, and calm
- **Signs of Imbalance:** Insomnia, difficulty concentrating or meditating, always feeling busy, lacking self-esteem
- **How to balance, heal, treat:** Try sunbathing, wear or visualize yellow, use neroli or Roman chamomile oils, practice the yogic front platform pose or sun salutations, hold citrine or sunstone, drink chamomile tea with lemon and honey

HEART CHAKRA

- **Location:** Middle of chest, heart region
- **Associations:** Compassion, love, healing, balance, forgiveness, trust, inner peace
- **Signs of Balance:** Feeling love, equanimity, compassion, harmony, and forgiveness
- **Signs of Imbalance:** Heart and lung issues, asthma, feeling apathy
- **How to balance, heal, treat:** Hug someone or cuddle with a pet, wear or visualize green, use rose or geranium oils, practice the yogic camel pose or warrior 1 pose, hold rose quartz or aventurine, practice breathwork

THROAT CHAKRA

- **Location:** Throat
- **Associations:** Communication, expression, feelings, belief systems, exchange of knowledge
- **Signs of Balance:** Feeling you can express your authentic self, healthy self-talk, being an active listener
- **Signs of Imbalance:** Throat issues, thyroid issues, TMJ, anxiety, fear of communicating or excessive talking, feeling unheard
- **How to balance, heal, treat:** Try singing, praying, or using mantras, wear or visualize blue, use lavender or rosemary oils, practice the yogic cobra pose or neck stretches, hold blue lace agate or kyanite, use hyssop or licorice lozenges

THIRD EYE CHAKRA

- **Location:** Between the brows
- **Associations:** Intuition, perception, psychic abilities, intellect, dreams
- **Signs of Balance:** Feeling focused, thoughtful, insightful, and intuitive
- **Signs of Imbalance:** Nightmares, headaches, issues with eyes and ears, personality disorders
- **How to balance, heal, treat:** Close your eyes and use your mind's eye to see yourself in your highest form, wear or visualize indigo/deep purple, use sandalwood or frankincense oils, practice the yogic child's pose, hold sodalite or lapis lazuli, remove fluoride from diet

CROWN CHAKRA

- **Location:** Crown of the head
- **Associations:** Wisdom, understanding, spirituality, divine connection, enlightenment
- **Signs of Balance:** Feeling a sense of purpose, feeling aware, spiritual, in touch with divinity and the universe
- **Signs of Imbalance:** Extreme sensitivity, not feeling self-aware, feeling disconnected
- **How to balance, heal, treat:** Try meditating, wear or visualize violet or silver, use frankincense or lotus oils, practice the yogic lotus pose or tree pose, hold labradorite or selenite

CHAKRA MEDITATION

This meditation can be done from two positions. The first is to sit with your legs crossed, sitting upright with your shoulders back so you are in a straight posture. Or, you may lie down on a flat surface (a little cushioning like a blanket or a yoga mat is recommended).

Close your eyes and take a few deep breaths to center yourself in the present moment. We will be moving through the chakras in this meditation, balancing them one by one, starting at the root.

Begin by visualizing a red ball of light glowing at the base of your spine. Notice this red light and recognize it as your root chakra. Envision this light glowing and pulsating. See it open like the petals of a flower and start to move in a clockwise direction. As it moves clockwise, envision this motion spinning gently like a pinwheel or a spiral. Know that as the red light gently spins clockwise, your root chakra is shifting into a healthy and balanced state.

Now visualize an orange ball of light glowing in your pelvic bowl. Notice this orange light and recognize it as your sacral chakra. Envision this light glowing and pulsating. See it open like the petals of a flower and start to move in a clockwise direction. As it moves clockwise, envision this motion spinning gently like a pinwheel or a spiral. Know that as the orange light gently spins clockwise, your sacral chakra is shifting into a healthy, balanced state.

Next, envision a yellow ball of light glowing below your breastbone. This yellow light is your solar chakra. Follow the process outlined above before moving to the next chakra.

Then, envision a green ball of light glowing in your chest by your heart. This green light is your heart chakra. Follow the process outlined above before moving to the next chakra.

Envision a blue ball of light glowing in your throat. This blue light is your throat chakra. Follow the process outlined above before moving to the next chakra.

Envision a purple ball of light glowing between your brows. This purple light is your third eye chakra. Follow the process outlined above before moving to the next chakra.

Finally, envision a silver or white ball of light glowing at the crown of your head. This silver or white light is your crown chakra. Follow the process outlined above before moving on to the next step.

Before closing, visualize the rainbow of light emanating from your chakras, all spinning with healthy balanced energy. When you are ready, open your eyes, and notice how you feel.

Chapter Two:
CRYSTALS FOR SELF-CARE: CRYSTAL HEALING AND MAGIC

Crystals (and other mineral stones) have always been favorite precious amulets of healers, light workers, and witches. Every crystal contains unique energies and properties that can be a support for a variety of needs.

An interesting exercise for finding stones that are best for you is to visit a local retail store that carries a variety of crystals. Browse the crystals and see if you are drawn to any in particular.

Below is a guide to crystals that have properties that work perfectly for the witch doing self-care work.

- **Amethyst:** Amethyst is used for tranquility, mental focus, wisdom, love magic, dreamwork, and psychic abilities. If you are feeling moody or angry, try holding this stone and saying the mantra, *"I feel internal peace and balance."*
- **Ametrine:** Ametrine is a mix of amethyst and citrine, and possesses the properties of both. As such, it's a

perfect stone for balancing yin and yang energies, cleansing the aura, and relieving tension. Ametrine also releases blocked energy and stimulates creativity. Keep ametrine with you when working on creative projects.

- **Apatite:** Apatite is a good meditation stone that enhances psychic abilities. It also boosts creativity and increases motivation for completing tasks. **Blue apatite** aids in stress relief, and promotes spiritual growth as well as expansion of knowledge.

- **Aquamarine:** Aquamarine is an excellent crystal for sensitive people to carry if they are feeling overwhelmed and want to feel a sense of security. This crystal supports spiritual development, active listening, clear communication, and a sense of independence. To feel the healing energy of the ocean, carry aquamarine with moonstone and ocean jasper.

- **Aventurine:** Aventurine lends optimism in new situations, fosters happiness, soothes nerves, offers protection from psychic vampires, and helps to heal heartbreak. **Green aventurine** can be used to help with growth and abundance magic. Write something you want to grow in your life on a small piece of paper, wrap a piece of aventurine in the paper, and bury it in your garden.

- **Blue Lace Agate:** Blue lace agate assists in speaking your truth, being heard, and communicating with the highest of intentions. Anoint a piece of blue lace agate with lavender essential oil and place on your throat chakra to support healthy self-talk.

- **Bloodstone:** Bloodstone purifies negativity, enhances courage, and strengthens spell work. Carry a piece of bloodstone and carnelian to feel strong, courageous, and empowered.

- **Calcite:** Calcite is often white, can be found in several other colors. It's a good stone for meditation, improving cognition, and connecting to spiritual aspects of self. Calcite also brings uplifting thoughts and helps neutralize negativity. **Orange calcite** renews stagnant energy and promotes an adventurous spirit. **Green calcite** can remove stress and replace it with self-compassion. If you are healing your heart, use green calcite to facilitate forgiveness and restore health.

- **Carnelian:** Carnelian is a stone of courage and passion. It lends energy and balance to the three lower chakras and can help with sexual empowerment. Anoint carnelian with amber and rose essential oils and carry with you to attract passion into your life.

- **Citrine:** Citrine can assist you with feeling mental clarity, awaken your imagination, and assist you in creative endeavors. It is also an excellent crystal to have on hand for boosting happiness and self-esteem. It can be used in magical spells to attract success and restore hope in your life. Keep a piece of citrine in your bowl of sugar to attract sweet success into your home.

- **Fluorite:** Fluorite comes in a very wide range of colors, all of which absorb negative energy and promote positive energy, making it a great cleansing crystal. This stone assists with focus and clarity, learning and retaining new information, inspiration, and increasing self-confidence. It can also be used to help deflect electromagnetic frequencies from electronic devices. **Green fluorite** can attract money and abundance, and promotes a calm state of mind.

- **Hematite:** Hematite is an anchoring crystal, grounding the energetic body and absorbing negativity. Hold after magical work or psychic work. Hematite is wonderful to keep at your desk if you work in a toxic work environment. It also works well in combination with obsidian and smoky quartz for protection and dealing with challenging emotions.
- **Howlite:** Howlite is a calming crystal to assist in developing spirituality, deepening your inner wisdom, and recalling your dreams. It is a soothing crystal that will help you if you need to cool down and eliminate stress.
- **Jade:** has a very calming energy, and is excellent help for unsettling situations in your life. To bring insights from the spiritual realm, place jade over your third eye. Keep a piece in your pocket to help recharge your energy and keep your immune system in good shape.
- **Kyanite:** Kyanite is a crystal of connection and spiritual ascension. Work with kyanite if you are healing karmic debts, or if you want to break through to see truths and reveal a better sense of self. Surround a dark blue candle with kyanite, labradorite, and sodalite when you are meditating to have a deeply meaningful session.
- **Labradorite:** Labradorite is a crystal of transformation, magic, and psychic abilities. This is an excellent stone to have during transitional times and will aid in healthy self-awareness. It is a favorite stone of witches and is said to help enhance psychic powers. Keep a piece of labradorite near you when doing divination readings.
- **Lapis Lazuli:** Lapis lazuli is a stone of higher guidance and intuition. It helps maintain connection with the higher self and access to inspiration from the spiritual

plane. Hold a piece of lapis to your third eye, or in your hand while meditating, to strengthen your ability to quickly identify what your truth is and give you the confidence to express it.

- **Lepidolite:** Lepidolite is a crystal of acceptance. It helps to release past trauma, relieve stress, clear blocked energy, and bring balance to a racing mind. Keep a piece of lepidolite on your altar to keep the space purified for love and peace.

- **Malachite:** Malachite supports spiritual growth and emotional courage, inspiring us to make important changes and take emotional risks. Work with this stone when releasing old emotional wounds, especially those suffered in childhood. Malachite also encourages expression of feelings, and promotes healthy, positive relationships and empathy for others.

- **Mookaite Jasper:** Mookaite jasper helps on spiritual journeys, assisting with self-discovery through sacred ritual and dreamwork. Wear this stone when visiting sacred and ancient sites to tap into the wisdom of these places. Mookaite can also boost self-esteem and help you find your tribe.

- **Moonstone:** Moonstone is a crystal of intuition, goddess energy, self-discovery, and psychic abilities. It is a magical stone that can be used in esbat and lunar magic. Go outside and stand under the light of the full moon, holding a piece of moonstone. Repeat the following three times: *"I feel the flow of peace and blessings in my life; I'm in a space to receive magical insight."* Keep the moonstone with you until the next full moon. **Peach moonstone** can be used to support self-compassion, comfort, and healing.

- **Moss Agate:** Moss agate is a healing stone that can bring calm and peace to your body. It is also a grounding stone that can help you stay balanced when facing changes in your life. If you are a gardener, this stone can help bring growth to your plants. Keep a piece by healing herbs in your garden to help amplify their energy.
- **Obsidian:** Obsidian will shed its light on blockages, helping you to clear up confusion and work through trauma. It is a strong protection stone and is especially protective against bullies and instigators. Rainbow obsidian can be used to align chakras and help you make a shift when feeling stuck.
- **Pyrite:** Pyrite, with its resemblance to gold, is a powerful stone for wealth and abundance magic. It is also a protective stone that strengthens confidence, improves memory, and helps relieve fatigue and mental sluggishness.
- **Quartz:** Quartz is a versatile mineral found in a variety of colors, each with its own magical properties. Both **clear and white quartz** promote healing, clarity, spiritual development, and are useful in meditation. Placing clear quartz in the bath is a good way to unwind and clear your mind when facing confusing events. **Rose quartz** is a crystal of gentle love that can reduce stress, frustration, and shame, and replace these energies with love, compassion, and kindness. **Smoky quartz** is an essential grounding stone for protection, earthing, and energetic cleansing, and releases grief and anger. **Tangerine quartz** energizes creative projects and promotes passion, curiosity, and playfulness.

- **Rhodochrosite:** Rhodochrosite is a stone of self-love and self-compassion. It heals the inner child and is an excellent stone for anyone who suffered from abuse or trauma—it can be worn as a pendant that rests on your heart chakra to continually assist in this healing. Rhodochrosite can also lift depression, enhance creativity, and mend friendships and love relationships. Use in spells related to peace and love.

- **Selenite:** Selenite clears and purifies energy, removes blockages, and can assist you in spiritual work. Many crystal healers wave wands of selenite over the body to smooth, calm, comfort, and purify auric energy. Use selenite with moonstone for lunar and goddess magic.

- **Sodalite:** Sodalite activates intuition and mental fortitude. Sodalite is a wonderful crystal for those seeking a sense of self in meditative work and magic. It removes confusion and reveals deep inner truths. **Sunset sodalite** is a gorgeous new discovery that contains veins of sunstone in it, lending support to self-esteem through positive and creative energy.

- **Tiger's Eye:** Tiger's eye is a stone of strength and vitality. It reinforces willpower and promotes success. It can be used in magic for security, protection, success, creativity, and animal communication. Place a yellow votive candle in the center of a fire-safe plate. To promote creative success, surround the candle with three pieces of tiger's eye and three pieces of citrine. Light the candle and say, "Creativity, imagination, success, and inspiration. I now create artistic and abundant manifestation." 🗓️

- **Tourmaline:** Tourmaline comes in a wide variety of colors, all of which can help ground spiritual energy, clear and balance the chakras, and help ease fear and anxiety. Many also associate tourmaline with luck and prosperity. **Black tourmaline** is used for protection, grounding, and banishing fear and negativity. **Green tourmaline** promotes strength, stamina, and vitality. **Pink tourmaline** can conjure up joy and happiness while allowing you to find solace and strength in your own vulnerability. It can be used to attract loving relationships into your life.

- <u>**Unakite:**</u> Unakite is a stone of deep emotional healing. Hold unakite when you are feeling angry to help release heavy emotions. It also assists in psychological healing and maturation.

CRYSTAL MAGIC FOR WELL-BEING

Crystals can be used in self-care magic in a variety of ways, from traditional spellcrafts to simply placing crystals strategically throughout your home. Below, you'll find ideas for incorporating crystals into sachets and jars, creating crystal grids, and other suggestions for harnessing the power of these stones to enhance your overall well-being.

CRYSTAL SACHET FOR GROUNDING BODY, MIND, AND SPIRIT

This is a small bag that you can hold or carry to feel grounded and anchored to the earth. If you don't have access to petrified wood or stones with fossils in them, tree bark will work fine. Just be sure to gather fallen bark from the ground—never pull bark from a living tree.

You will need:
- Small brown pouch
- Pinch of dirt
- An acorn
- Petrified wood, fossil rock, or tree bark
- 1 or more pieces moss agate
- 1 or more pieces smoky quartz

- Cedarwood essential oil
- Patchouli essential oil

Instructions:

Combine the dirt, acorn, petrified wood, moss agate, and smoky quartz in a small bowl.

Put a couple drops of each essential oil on top of the combined contents.

Using your hands, continue to mix the contents around, so that the oil is in contact with each of the items in the bowl. With your mind's eye, visualize the contents glowing green and brown. When the contents are warm from the energy in your fingers, place them in the pouch and tie it shut.

Hold the pouch in your hands and say the following:

"Dirt, stone, grass, and trees, this pouch helps to ground me. Like an anchor I'm connected to Earth, who keeps me balanced, safe, and secure."

Note: if you're able, try charging this sachet outdoors, with your bare feet on the ground, for an added boost of earth energy.

CRYSTAL SACHET TO HEAL A BROKEN HEART

Mending a broken heart. takes time, but a little magical TLC can help ease the process. Hold or carry this sachet with you to support you in grieving the loss of a relationship. Use as many pieces of each stone as you like—just be sure not to keep the bag's weight on the lighter side.

You will need:

- Small pink pouch
- 1 tsp. dried marjoram herbs
- 1 tsp. dried lavender buds
- Heart Healing Oil (see Chapter Four)
- Green calcite
- Pink tourmaline
- Rose quartz
- Aventurine

Instructions:

Combine the herbs and crystals in a small bowl.

Put a couple drops of the Healing Heart Oil on top of the crystals and herbs.

Using your hands, continue to mix the contents around, so that the oil is in contact with each of the items in the bowl. With your mind's eye, visualize the contents growing pink and green. When the contents are warm from the energy in your fingers, place them in the pouch and tie it shut.

Hold the pouch in your hands and say the following:

"Healed heart, whole heart, blessings from these crystals and plants. Allow love and joy to flow through me again."

Note: If you like, recharge your sachet whenever you want more support. Light a pink or white candle, repeat the step above, and place the sachet in front of the candle for a little while, or until the candle burns out.

LUCKY 7 GRATITUDE JAR TO ATTRACT ABUNDANCE AND BLESSINGS

This gratitude jar is something you can work with regularly to remind yourself of the blessings you have in your life and the dreams you wish to manifest. It would work really well on your self-care altar (see "Setting Up a Self-Care Altar" in the Introduction). The jar should fit all of the items below, leaving half the jar free to fill with notes of gratitude (described below).

You will need:

- A large mason jar
- 1 piece pyrite
- 1 piece aventurine
- 1 piece citrine
- 1 piece tiger's eye
- 1 piece jade
- 1 piece malachite
- 1 piece green tourmaline
- Several coins
- Dried beans and/or large seeds
- Green rice
- Any other personal amulets that represent abundance and blessings
- Small slips of paper

Instructions:

Line the bottom of the jar with a layer of green rice. Next, add the seeds and beans, then the coins. Then add in the crystals.

Hold the jar and say the following incantation:

"I am blessed seven days a week, I have gratitude for what is in my life. This jar conjures prosperity and wealth, sevenfold with each offering I make it. So mote it be."

Place the jar in a special place where you can work with it. Using a small slip of paper, write down something that you are thankful for. Fold the slip up and say:

"I am thankful for this blessing in my life. I am grateful for what I have and what I will manifest."

Give these offerings of gratitude daily for best results.

When your jar is full, open it and look through a few (or all) of the notes of gratitude. Spend some time reflecting on how your overall abundance has grown since you created the jar. If you like, choose a few notes to keep in the jar, and make room for new offerings of gratitude by recycling the rest.

CRYSTAL BOWL FOR THE TOXIC WORKPLACE

If you are currently working at a job that is uncomfortable and toxic, this bowl is something you can keep discreetly on your desk to ward off negative energies and less-than-collaborative co-workers. (Be sure to also visit your HR department if things are seriously uncomfortable.)

You will need:

- A pinch of sea salt
- 1 tsp dried basil (or a few fresh leaves)
- 1 tsp dried rosemary (or a dried sprig)
- 1 or more pieces of the following crystals: hematite, obsidian, smoky quartz, tiger's eye, and/or black

tourmaline, and any other stones that are protective talismans for you.
- 1 piece green aventurine
- 1 piece citrine
- 1 piece rose quartz (optional)
- 1 piece howlite (optional)

Instructions:

Make a small tea with the sea salt, basil, and rosemary. Allow it to steep until you can smell the herbs and the water is cool to the touch. Using your fingers, dab the tea onto the bottom of a small bowl. You don't need to use a large amount—just enough to be able to move your finger easily through and around the bowl.

Trace the bowl's rim in a clockwise direction with your finger and say the following:

"I am protected, I am safe, I am guarded from my toxic workplace."

Repeat this incantation three times and then draw a pentacle onto the bottom of the bowl.

Add the protective crystals to the bowl. Also add a piece of green aventurine and citrine to ensure that you do not block success or opportunities. If you'd like to add rose quartz and howlite, this will allow you to feel compassion and patience at work.

If you'd like, you can anoint the crystals with the tea. Just make sure you do not get softer crystals and stones wet, as they will dissolve.

When your crystals are in place, say the following incantation:

"I am thankful for prosperity and success. I am protected from all negativity at work. This bowl is a shield, allowing me to rise above that which could harm me. So mote it be!"

Bring the bowl home from work periodically to cleanse it. You can leave it out in moonlight or sunlight, ring a bell over it, or pass it through the smoke from incense or an herbal smoking wand.

CRYSTALS PLACED IN THE HOME

You can place crystals around your home to generate specific energies. If you have ever been in a room or a home with many crystals, you know that they can make a space feel vibrant with healing energy. If you are looking to bring specific types of energy into your home life, consider the following:

- **For a protected home:** Place pieces of smoky quartz, hematite, and/or obsidian on your windowsills and above your doorways. You can also bury pieces of these crystals at the corners of your property.

- **For a home of happiness:** Keep citrine points in an area that allows them to capture the sunlight. Keep selenite wands above doorways to balance and purify energy.

- **For a home that attracts love:** Keep rose quartz and amethyst by your bed.

- **For a home that attracts abundance:** Keep pyrite where you store your money or credit cards. Keep a piece of jade with your bills. Have a place on your altar where you collect coins in a jar with pieces of aventurine.

- **To build up magical energy in your home:** Create crystal grids in areas where you perform magic or do spiritual work. Circle your home with quartz crystal points. Keep labradorite and lapis lazuli around your magical items or books.

- **To create a create a home of good health:** Keep green calcite or green tourmaline in your medicine cabinet and a piece of bloodstone with your first aid kit. Keep a piece of blue apatite at your kitchen table. Wear jade or keep a piece by your bed.

- **To have powerful dreams:** Place amethyst, moonstone, and sodalite by your bed or under your bed.

ZEN GARDEN FOR SPIRITUAL WISDOM

Miniature Zen gardens are easily created from scratch with a large display dish and sand (though you can find ready-made kits for purchase as well). To create a Zen garden with the theme of Spiritual Wisdom, add moonstone, labradorite, howlite, and kyanite.

If you wish, you may also add larger chunks of myrrh or frankincense resin. Using a wooden Zen garden rake, move the crystals around and create various images or designs, allowing your mind to quiet and your spirit to guide you.

CRYSTAL GRIDS

Crystal grids are created by laying out certain crystals in a specific geometric pattern in order to amplify energy associated with a magical goal. Crystal grids can be set up in a smaller space, such as on your altar, or given larger space such as on the floor of a room.

Allow your crystal grid to sit for as long as you like—the longer you allow it to sit, the more powerful the energy will be. Make a practice of spending a few moments each day near the grid, and observe any energetic or intuitive sensations you pick up. When you are ready to release the energy into your space, you can open the grid by moving the outer crystal points to face outwards.

Note: With the exception of crystal points, the shapes depicted in the graphs below are merely to differentiate the various crystals that are being used – any shapes, tumbled or raw will do.

CRYSTAL GRID TO PROMOTE SELF-LOVE

This grid requires a large number of crystals, but it can be very powerful in generating a feeling of self-love. When you set up the crystal points, make sure that they are pointing in a clockwise direction.

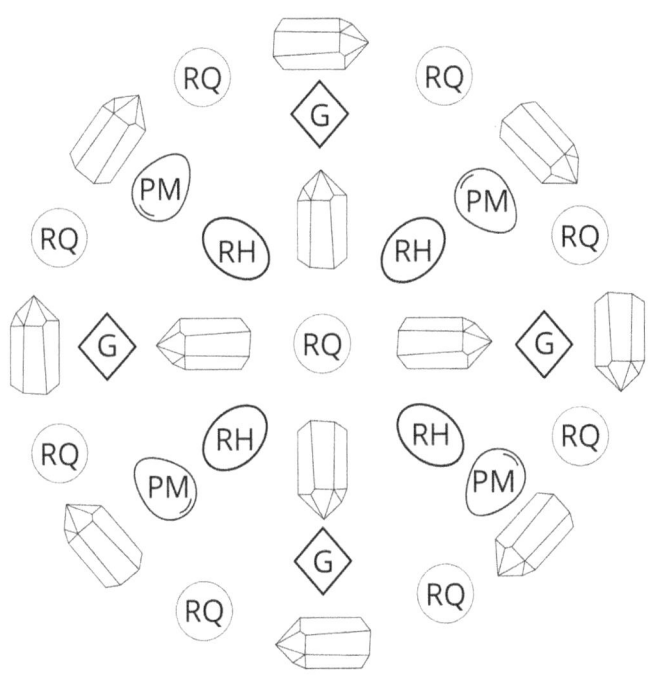

KEY:
RQ = Rose quartz **RH** = Rhodochrosite
G = Green calcite **PM** = Peach moonstone
Crystals = Quartz crystal points

CALMING CRYSTAL GRID TO PROMOTE PEACEFUL SELF-CARE

This is another large grid, but it will generate powerful energies to promote peace of mind when you are focusing on self-care. When you set up the crystal points, make sure that they are pointing in a clockwise direction.

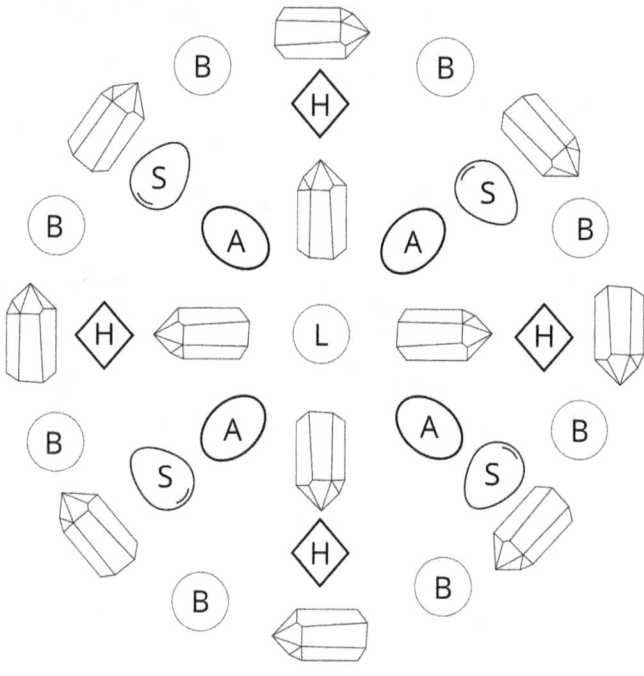

KEY:

H = Howlite **B** = Blue lace agate
A = Amethyst **S** = Sodalite
L = Lepidolite **Crystals** = Quartz crystal points

GOLDEN RATIO SPIRAL GRID FOR CREATIVE INSPIRATION

This special crystal grid follows the line of the golden ratio, and is designed to awaken artistic creativity and inspiration. Each of these colorful crystals is associated with creativity, conjuring inspiration, hearing divine guidance, and conjuring artistic beauty. While the crystals within the spiral can be any shape or form, it is recommended that the beginning and ending crystals be points.

After you set up the grid, light yellow candles in your workspace and diffuse sweet orange and sandalwood oils. You may also say the following mantra: "I am an artist; I express divine creativity; I am inspired; my art is magical."

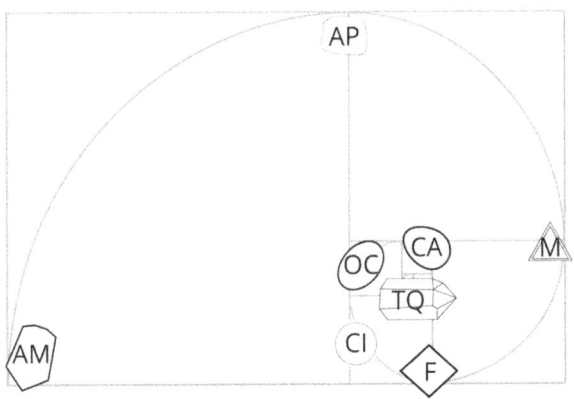

KEY:

TQ = Tangerine quartz
OC = Orange calcite
F = Green fluorite
AP = Blue apatite

CA = Carnelian
CI = Citrine
M = Malachite
AM = Ametrine

Chapter Three:
SELF-CARE FOR THE KITCHEN WITCH: MAGICAL FOODS TO NOURISH YOUR SOUL

In this chapter we'll examine how a witch can practice magical self-care in the realm of food, beverages, and the act of cooking. There is the old saying that "we are what we eat," so this chapter will focus on harnessing the magic of healthy and nourishing foods.

When our body is working with optimal "fuel," we not only feel and look better, but our mind functions better and our mood improves. What's more, our magical work is more potent, as we're drawing on stronger and more balanced personal power.

Food, like everything else in the universe, has its own energy, and its own vibrational frequency. This energy—known as *prana* in Hindu tradition, and as *chi* in many Asian cultures—is the life force that runs through every living thing on Earth, including plants, animals, and even water.

Fresh foods, especially fruits and vegetables, have a high life-force energy, and so are considered high-vibrational foods. On the other end of the spectrum are highly processed snack foods (which are called "junk food" for a reason!) and even microwave-ready meals, which may contain some nutritious ingredients, but have been through so much processing that the life force has largely been extracted by the time you eat them.

Consider the difference between steamed vegetables and deep-fried vegetables. While the latter may be more appealing, depending on your personal preferences, the steamed version is definitely going to have a lighter impact on your digestion, resulting in a "cleaner," more high-frequency feeling after you eat. This is because, as a cooking method, steaming allows the vegetables to preserve more of their prana (or chi), whereas deep frying reduces this energy.

"We are what we eat" is literally true—every nutrient the body takes in and metabolizes becomes physically part of the body's cellular structure. At the energy level, we take into our bodies the prana or chi of each ingredient in our food, which merges into our personal life force energy.

Nutritional magic means supporting your body's health through a sacred, plant-positive, and colorful diet centered around fresh, living foods. While the occasional decadent meal or dessert can be a delight to indulge in, maintaining a healthy diet based on your body's needs will allow for you to maintain healthy physical wellness.

This chapter will provide tips for improving your overall diet, as well as the magical properties of several key foods, advice for preparing meals with a magical self-care mindset, and a few easy recipes to get you started.

NUTRITIONAL MAGIC: ALCHEMY: MAKING POSITIVE CHANGES FOR BODY, MIND, AND SPIRIT

Food can be a very emotional experience. Letting go of certain pleasures, such as fast food or sugary snacks, can feel like a painful sacrifice at first. If this is something you struggle with, consider creating a ritual of offering up your "bad food habits" in order to honor your body. The days leading up to the new moon are an ideal time frame for this kind of working.

No matter your situation, the best approach to improving your overall nutritional health is to pay attention to your own body, and make gradual changes rather than aiming for a thorough overhaul all at once. Try replacing one unhealthy food at a time with a more nutritious alternative. For example, if you like a lot of sugar in your coffee, try substituting with honey or stevia extract.

Note: If this chapter inspires you to make significant changes to your food choices, you may want to consider consulting a nutritionist, naturopathic doctor, or other holistic health care practitioner for advice tailoring your diet to your body's needs. It's important to recognize that no two bodies will respond the same way to any given diet. For example, some people function optimally on a vegan diet, while others thrive with the Paleo approach.

You may also find that certain restrictions (such as allergies, intolerances, other health issues, or even budget concerns) mean that you must find creative ways to be mindful about what you consume. Do the best you can with the suggestions in this chapter, but ultimately, do what works for you.

Quick Tips for Magical Shifts in Your Diet:

If the body is a temple, then what offerings provide it the best opportunity to conjure real-life powerful magic? Here are some relatively simple ways to start boosting your own life force with nourishing, magical foods:

- Eat the rainbow—in other words, eat colorful fresh fruits and vegetables in a variety of colors. Different colors signify different nutrients, so the more variety of colors you eat, the more well-rounded the benefits your body receives will be.

- Use spices like cinnamon, turmeric, garlic, and ginger in your cooking. These powerful foods help fight cancer, promote healthy heart function and blood circulation, reduce inflammation, and provide a host of other health benefits.

- Find healthy snack replacements. For example, try eating almonds or carrots instead of chips, or peanut butter on apples instead of a candy bar. There are also plenty of recipes online for healthier versions of time-honored favorites like chocolate, cookies, and even chips.

- Use healthier oils, if at all—coconut oil, extra virgin olive oil, avocado, and organic peanut oil are considered healthier varieties than corn, canola, safflower, or "vegetable" oil.

- Use healthier sweeteners, if at all—honey, maple syrup, monk fruit, stevia, and coconut sugar are considered healthier alternatives to cane sugar.

- Replace processed grains with whole and ancient grains—some of the healthiest grains include brown rice, barley, quinoa, rolled oats, millet, and farro.

NUTRITIOUS FOODS AND SPICES AND THEIR MAGICAL CORRESPONDENCES

There are many ways to identify the magical properties of a given food. One way is to look at the folklore about the food and how it was historically revered and honored. Another way is to consider how the food looks and feels—that is, to ponder how its color, shape, and flavor speaks to you about its unique energetic qualities. You may also want to see how your body responds to specific food to see if it something that is particularly energetically suited for you.

All of the foods listed here are considered healthy and nourishing. Many are called "superfoods" because they are packed with vitamins, minerals, antioxidants, which are vital to helping your body stay healthy. While this list focuses on magical energies rather than specific nutritional benefits, know that incorporating as many of these foods into your diet as possible may be the most important step you can take in your self-care journey.

- **Acai:** Acai is a berry that can be used for love and beauty magic. Acai is a sacred food to the indigenous tribes living near the Amazon, where it originates.

- **Almonds:** Almonds are connected to the element of Air, making them useful in magic for intellect and communication. They are also used in money and healing magic.
- **Apples:** In Celtic mythology, apples were connected to the Otherworld, while in ancient Greece, the apple was associated with Aphrodite, the goddess of love. Apples are used in love and health magic. They are also a popular food to use for divination at Samhain.
- **Apricots:** Apricots are used in love and peace magic, their color infusing creative passion into the world and helping you do what you love to do.
- **Arugula:** Arugula, along with other greens on this list, is helpful in healing, abundance, and fertility magic. It's also known as "rocket," making it a go-to-green for when you need a quick turn-around in your magical work.
- **Avocado:** Avocado can be used in love and beauty magic. You can use the pit in love and passion spells. They can also be used in spells to help conjure self-love, especially for those who feel tough on the outside and soft on the inside.
- **Bananas:** Due to their shape, it's probably no surprise that bananas are used for fertility magic, but they can also be used to conjure prosperity. Bananas are sacred in Hinduism and banana leaves can be an offering to the god Ganesh.
- **Barley:** Barley can be used for money, prosperity, and healing magic. Barley is an ancient grain that was honored by Sumerians, Egyptians, Hebrews, Greeks, and Romans as a means of sustenance. Therefore,

barley is also a symbol of security and having our basic needs met.

- **Beans:** Beans of all kinds are used for attraction and prosperity magic.
- **Beets:** Beets are an earthing, grounding root vegetable that can be used in love and beauty magic. Perhaps it's the root's red, heart-like shape that connects beets to romantic magic.
- **Bell and Hot Peppers:** Hot peppers are excellent for protection or quickening magic. However, bell peppers are a little more mellow on the palette, and therefore they can be associated with magic for empowerment and healthy boundaries.
- **Blueberries:** Blueberries are supportive in calming, supportive, and nurturing magic. Blueberries were revered by Native Americans, who said they were "star berries" sent from Great Spirit to feed hungry children during famine. Therefore, they are a sacred fruit, representing divine sustenance and connection.
- **Broccoli:** Broccoli can be used in healing magic, especially for regaining strength.
- **Cacao:** Cacao is used for love and comfort spells. Cacao was sacred to the ancient Mayans, who believed that it was a gift from the gods. There is no disagreement that chocolate, which is made from cacao, is a divine indulgence.
- **Carrots:** Carrots can be used in fertility and abundance magic. The carrot has long been revered as a healing vegetable and can be used to reconnect with the healing energies of the Earth element.

- **Chia Seeds:** Chia seeds can be used in abundance and prosperity magic.
- **Chickpeas:** Chickpeas are used for growth and abundance magic.
- **Cinnamon:** Cinnamon is associated with the sun and the element of Fire due to its warming effect. It is often used in success and prosperity magic, and to speed up or add power to spellwork in general. Cinnamon can also enhance psychic abilities—add a little cinnamon to your coffee or tea to awaken your sixth sense.
- **Dates:** Dates are used to focus on spirituality and assist in magical empowerment. Paintings of date palms decorated the walls of Solomon's temple and dates are a sacred food in the Quran.
- **Flax Seeds:** Flaxseeds are used for growth and abundance magic. Flax seeds are so ancient that archeologists have discovered flax fibers from 30,000 years ago in a cave in the modern-day nation of Georgia.
- **Garlic:** Garlic can be used in endurance and protection magic. Garlic may be best known for its protective powers, due in part to the folklore that says it keeps away vampires. Garlic has been cultivated for over 5,000 years, dating as far back as ancient Egypt where it was worshiped for warding off evil as well as increasing strength.
- **Ginger:** Ginger gives energy and power to spells and can also be used for courage and success magic. It also gives a lusty boost to romance, and as such is used in many love spells.
- **Grapefruit:** Grapefruit is used for happiness, healing and purification magic.

- **Green Peas:** Green peas are used in love and healing magic.
- **Honey:** Raw honey is known to sweeten magical spells. It can bring a gentle and positive vibration to food magic. It can also be used to connect to Fae spirits and enhance spiritual connection with divine forces.
- **Kale:** Kale is best used for money and healing magic.
- **Kiwi:** Kiwi is used for fertility, love, and growth magic.
- **Lemons:** Lemons are used in love and purification magic. They can also bring light and cheery energy to a situation, and can be used in spells to attract friendship.
- **Lentils:** Lentils can be used in comfort and peace magic.
- **Mushrooms:** Mushrooms can be used in spiritual magic and can assist in awakening psychic abilities. Their energies can foster heavenly and earthly balance.
- **Papaya:** Papaya can be used for sensuality, goddess, love, and beauty magic.
- **Pumpkin Seeds:** Pumpkin seeds can be used in growth, abundance, and fertility magic. They are also a wonderful symbol of transformation, so if you are looking to transform your financial situation into something greater, be sure to add pumpkin seeds to your spell.
- **Quinoa:** Quinoa is used in growth and abundance magic. Quinoa is a sacred grain for the Incan cultures of Peru, where it was said to be a gift from the stars.
- **Raspberries:** Raspberries are used for happiness, protection, feminine, and faery magic.

- **Rice:** Rice is used for money and fertility magic. Scatter dry jade rice (or white rice mixed with a bit of green food coloring) around your place of business or keep a small pouch of it with you to ensure prosperity.

- **Spinach:** Spinach is used in money and healing magic. Because of its iron content, you may also want to consider using spinach in healing spells that help to restore the body to strength after periods of illness or a difficult injury.

- **Strawberries:** Strawberries are used in love, fertility, and faery magic.

- **Sunflower Seeds:** Sunflower seeds are used for success, power, and protection magic.

- **Sweet Potato:** Sweet potatoes can be used in magic to grow love, happiness, and pleasure.

- **Tangerines:** Tangerines can empower a spell with brightness, swiftness, and intelligence.

- **Tempeh:** Tempeh is used for growth, stability, and security magic.

- **Vanilla bean:** Vanilla bean's sweet, mellow flavor can be used in love magic, or to smooth out excess mental energy. This spice is connected to the Water element.

- **Watermelon:** Watermelon can be used in healing magic, especially if you are trying to cool, calm, or revitalize your spirits.

- **Walnuts:** Walnuts are used for empowerment, encouragement, wisdom, and mental agility magic.

PREPARING MAGICAL RECIPES

As discussed earlier, the quality of what we eat is determined by the quality of the energy inherent in the food, as well as the way in which it's prepared. Whether you're making a meal for a specific magical intention, or simply to take good care of your body, your own vibrational frequency during the process has an effect on the results.

If you find yourself feeling heavy or unpleasant in any way after a meal, reflect on how it was prepared. Were you eating at a restaurant where the employees are unhappy? If you ate at home, what was your state of mind like while you were cooking—were you feeling stressed or other negative emotions?

Make a point of creating as much ease and joy as you can during meal preparation. Put on music you enjoy, keep some cheerful crystals nearby, and/or light a candle to initiate good cooking vibrations. If the kitchen needs a good energetic cleansing, burn purifying incense or essential oils, or use the White Light Spray in Chapter 4.

Another important aspect of kitchen witchery is charging your ingredients, just as you would do for items used in a spell. The act of charging is meant to awaken your food's natural energies and fill it with intentions for wellness and vitality. When you charge food, you imbue it with gratitude and life-giving energy, showing thanks for the nutrition and asking for good health in return.

One simple way to do this is to get out all the ingredients you'll be using and charge them all at once. Hold your hands over them, palms down, and visualize each ingredient glowing with nourishing energy. Focus on your intentions for this meal—you may have a specific magical purpose in mind, or you may just want to focus on optimizing the benefits your body will receive from the food.

Finally, just before you eat, remember to bless your meal. I like to hold my hands over the food I am about to eat or place my hands on the bowl or dish the food is in. Close your eyes and envision the food growing with energy. Smell the food—as you breathe in, envision the food sending nutrients to any parts of the body you wish to give special attention to. Say the following incantation or create a personal one that shows your gratitude for its power:

"This food is a blessing and is a part of divinity, as I am a part of divinity. Within this food there is magic, and this magic will fill me with nutrition and health. I am in deep gratitude for this food, and with my words imbue it with the magical vibrations of divinity."

You can use this incantation before enjoying the recipes below, or if you like, create your own that's tailored toward the specific main ingredients of the dish or beverage. The first two recipes are spells in and of themselves—you can use the incantations there as models for each of the recipes that follow.

GOOD MORNING COFFEE SPELL

Bring a little pleasure into your morning cup of coffee. Brew your coffee as you normally would, pour it into a large mug, and add milk or creamer, if desired. Then add a teaspoon of cinnamon and sweeten with honey instead of sugar (if you like your coffee sweetened). Blend with a spoon, stirring clockwise. Say the following incantation:

"My day is energized with magic and success; this morning coffee makes me feel my best."

Take a moment to visualize your upcoming day going in the best possible direction. Repeat the incantation two more times, then enjoy your coffee!

GOLDEN MILK SELF-GROWTH SPELL

Golden milk is a popular warm beverage for its variety of healing properties. The ingredients are anti-inflammatory and full of antioxidants, and can help improve mood and circulation. Many people will enjoy a mug of golden milk at the end of a long day to rest and relax. This spell combines the health benefits of the beverage with your intentions on self-growth. This recipe makes one large mug of golden milk.

You will need:

- 1 cup light coconut milk (canned)
- 1 cup almond milk, unsweetened
- 1 ½ tsp. turmeric
- ½ tsp. ginger

- ½ tsp. cinnamon
- 1/8 tsp. cardamom (optional)
- 1/8 tsp. vanilla paste, or vanilla bean (optional)
- 1 tsp. coconut oil
- Dash of black pepper
- 1-2 tsp. honey, to taste

Instructions:

Put the milks in a small saucepan and heat on a medium-high heat.

Add the spices to the saucepan. Blend in coconut oil and honey.

Whisk frequently or use a hand blender to create a soft, foamy texture.

When the milk is ready, pour it into a large mug. Hold the mug in your hands while saying the following words:

"I heal, and I am wise. I grow and cultivate success in my life. May this golden milk bring me success and allow me to see where I grow best."

ENERGY AND DETOX SUN-BREWED TEA

This tea is meant to be brewed in the warmth of the sun. Allow it to awaken positive, empowered energy within you, all while assisting in digestion, circulation, and boosting your immune system. Be sure to use only purified, spring, or well-filtered tap water, as leaving water to warm in the sun can cause bacterial growth.

You will need:

- 8 to 10 cups of purified water or spring water

- 1 thinly sliced lemon
- 1 thinly sliced orange
- 1 to 2 tbsp. apple cider vinegar (with 'The Mother" culture)
- ¼ to ½ tsp. cayenne pepper
- ¼ to ½ inch of freshly grated ginger root
- Honey to taste (optional)
- Yerba mate tea bag for an extra boost (optional)
- Large glass pitcher

Instructions:

Place the lemon, orange, apple cider vinegar, cayenne pepper, ginger root, and optional ingredients into the bottom of the pitcher. Slowly stir in the water.

Cover the pitcher and place out in the sunlight. Allow it to brew for at least one hour, but no more than four hours. You can also surround the pitcher with pieces of orange calcite, tangerine quartz, and/or citrine crystal.

Refrigerate the tea and/or add ice if you want to drink it cold. This sun-brewed tea is best drunk prior to noon.

RELAXING MOON-BREWED TEA

This tea is meant to be brewed under the moonlight in the evening hours when you are ready to conclude your day. Its ingredients will align you with the magic of the moon, all while making you feel relaxed and at ease.

You will need:

- 7 to 8 cups room-temperature purified or spring water
- 1 to 2 cups coconut water

- Fresh blueberries
- Fresh cucumber slices
- 3 tsp. dried butterfly pea flower
- 2 tsp. dried lavender
- Handful of fresh lemon balm
- Honey to taste (optional)

Instructions:

Place the blueberries, cucumber, and dried herbs into the bottom of the pitcher. Slowly stir in the water and coconut water, and add a little honey if desired.

Cover the pitcher and allow to brew for at least one hour, but no more than four hours. If possible, place under the full moonlight. You can also surround the pitcher with pieces of moonstone, amethyst, and lapis lazuli.

Refrigerate the tea and/or add ice if you want to drink it cold. This moon brewed tea is best drunk after the sun sets.

ACAI BREAKFAST BOWL FOR SELF-LOVE

This bowl provides a sweet and healthy start to your day. The ingredients promote soothing, loving vibrations and a mellow mood. This recipe makes one bowl:

You will need:

- 1 3.5 oz. packet of frozen blended acai
- ½ cup watermelon, cut
- ½ cup frozen strawberries
- ½ cup granola, unsweetened
- 1 kiwi, peeled and sliced
- ¼ cup blueberries
- ¼ cup raspberries
- ½ avocado, sliced

- 1 tbsp. coconut flakes, unsweetened
- 1 tbsp. cacao chips
- Raw honey to taste (optional)

Instructions:

Blend the acai, watermelon, and strawberries in a high-speed blender for about 20 seconds. Pour into a large bowl.

Pour the granola on top of the blended fruit.

Assemble the raspberries, blueberries, kiwi, and avocado around the granola.

Top with coconut flakes and cacao chips. If you'd like a little touch of sweetness, drizzle a small amount of raw honey over the top.

BLISSFUL TROPICAL SMOOTHIE

This smoothie is buzzing with good vibrations and will blissfully connect you to the spirit of Aloha. The orange and yellow fruits can help bring energy to your sacral and solar chakras. The ingredients are also bright and happy, helping you to find your daily moment of bliss. If you can't find quality fresh fruits, substitute any of the below for their organic frozen counterparts. This recipe makes one large glass.

You will need:

- 1 ½ cups combination of nectarine, peach, mango, pineapple, and papaya (or a section from each)
- 1 peeled clementine
- 1 cup almond milk or coconut milk

- 2 tsp. coconut flakes (unsweetened)
- 1 tsp. bee pollen
- 1 tsp. ground flaxseed
- Raw honey to taste (optional)

Instructions:

Blend all of the ingredients in a high-speed blender for about 30 seconds. It's then ready to serve!

BUDDHA BOWL FOR ABUNDANCE

Buddha bowls are a fun way to playfully add all sorts of nutritious ingredients into one meal. This bowl is meant to support you in finding abundance and prosperity. There are several different steps to building this Buddha bowl, but it is delicious and nutritious. This recipe makes one bowl.

You will need:

- 1 cup of quinoa, barley, or farro
- 1 cup yellow squash or acorn squash, cubed
- 2-4 tsp. cooking oil (olive or coconut are recommended)
- Pinch of onion powder
- Sea salt and black pepper to taste
- 2 cups spinach
- 2 tbsp + 3-4 tbsp vegetable broth
- 1 clove garlic, minced
- ½ 15 oz can of pinto beans
- 1 tsp. dried thyme
- 1 tsp. dried sage
- Pinch of flaxseed meal or corn starch
- ½ cup tempeh

Instructions:

Cook the grains as the package directs. You can do this while prepping other parts of the recipe. Set the grains aside when done. If you like, surround the bowl they are sitting in with pyrite and jade.

For the squash: Preheat the oven to 375 degrees F. Cut the squash into cubes and dress evenly with 1-2 tsp. cooking oil. Sprinkle on onion powder, sea salt, and pepper. Bake for about 10 minutes, or until tender.

For the spinach: Heat a small pan over medium-high heat and put in 1-2 tsp. cooking oil. Once heated, add garlic and reduce temperature. Pour in 2 tbsp. vegetable broth and cook until steaming. Add the spinach and cover for 1 minute. Turn off heat, but keep covered.

For the pinto beans: Rinse and drain the beans. In a small saucepan, combine the remaining vegetable broth, sage, thyme, and flaxseed meal or corn starch. Stirring frequently, bring to a boil. Add the pinto beans, cover, and reduce heat to a simmer until ready to dish.

For the tempeh: Cut tempeh into ½-inch cubes and steam for five minutes. Set aside.

Assemble the meal by placing the grains in the bottom of the bowl. Place the squash, spinach, and tempeh on top of the grains, in each of their own equal sections. Top with the pinto beans.

CHAKRA BALANCING RAINBOW SALAD

This colorful salad is packed with nutrients, but also lends a hand in balancing the energy of all of the chakras. The

Blueberry Vinaigrette Dressing is not only divinely perfect for topping off this salad, but can be used on any tossed salad—just double the recipe. (It can be kept in the refrigerator for about a week.)

This recipe creates two large salads. Following the directions below, split the salad ingredients equally between both bowls.

You will need:

For the salad:

- ¼ cup beets, shredded
- 2 tbsp. red onion, thinly sliced
- 1 carrot, diced
- ¼ cup chickpeas (rinsed and drained if canned) OR ¼ cup fresh corn
- 1 -1 ½ cups baby spinach (or a variety of greens)
- ¼ cup cucumber, diced into small pieces
- ¼ cup purple cabbage, shredded
- ½ cup baby portobello mushrooms, cleaned and sliced
- 1 tbsp. crushed walnuts
- 1 tbsp. sunflower seeds

For the Blueberry Vinaigrette Dressing:

- 2 ½ tbsp. blueberries
- ½ tbsp. olive oil (or avocado oil, or vegetable broth)
- ½ tbsp. purified water
- 1 tbsp. white vinegar
- ½ tbsp. balsamic vinegar
- 2 tbsp. blueberries
- 1 tsp. honey (optional)
- ½ tsp. dried oregano

Instructions:

Place the baby spinach and/or greens into the bottom of each bowl.

Assemble the beets, red onion, carrot, chickpeas, cucumber, cabbage, and mushrooms on top of the beds of spinach to create a rainbow pattern.

Top with walnuts and sunflower seeds.

For the dressing, blend all of the ingredients on high until smooth. Dress the salads and serve.

MATCHA GREEN TEA POTION FOR SELF-COMPASSION

Feeling compassion for yourself means that you've identified your emotions and are tender with yourself in the pursuit of seeking wellness. This green tea potion will support your heart chakra and fill you with a peaceful sense of self-compassion. This recipe makes one large mug.

You will need:

- 1 tsp. matcha green tea powder
- 1 ¼ cups almond milk or coconut milk
- 1 tsp. rose petals
- 1 tsp. tulsi leaf
- Pinch of vanilla bean
- cooking thermometer

Instructions:

Place matcha green tea powder into a mug. Set aside.

Pour the milk into a small saucepan and heat slowly on medium.

Stir the milk frequently with a whisk. Add the herbs to the milk. (You can add them in a muslin tea bag or strain them from the milk after it has heated up.)

Continue to stir frequently with the whisk. Watch the temperature closely with a thermometer, as matcha green tea is best at 175 degrees Fahrenheit. One it reaches 175 degrees, remove from the heat.

Slowly pour the milk into the mug, whisking as you do to create a froth.

Chapter Four:
ENCHANTING SELF-CARE: AROMATHERAPY, BATH, AND BEAUTY MAGIC

While pampering and luxurious practices are not the foundation of self-care, they can still be valuable for showing yourself love, deepening your magical growth, and improving your overall well-being. This chapter focuses on bath, beauty, and therapeutic creations made from essential oils and other natural ingredients. These recipes are imbued with magic, and are here to support you along your journey of self-care.

There are a few important notes of caution to mention before moving forward here. Please be mindful about putting essential oils on your skin. We all have different skin types, and it's important to realize that while the ingredients in the formulas below tend to be safe for most skin types, some may not work for you. With very few exceptions, essential oils should be diluted in a carrier oil, such as olive, coconut, jojoba, sweet almond, grapeseed, or avocado oil.

While there isn't a standard, tried-and-true dilution ratio that's ideal for every single essential oil, most reputable sources advise a range of 5-15 drops of oil per ounce (or 2 tablespoons) of carrier oil. (Recipes may vary based on personal preferences, the specific types of essential oil(s) used, and/or the purpose of the recipe).

Furthermore, if you have sensitive skin or allergies, you need to be extra careful. Please do a patch test of any oil you haven't worked with before prior to using it on your skin. Dilute a drop of the essential oil in a half-teaspoon of carrier oil, then dab a cotton swab in the blend and apply it to your inner wrist or behind your knee. Place a waterproof adhesive bandage over the spot and leave in place for 24 hours. If any irritation occurs, remove the bandage and wash the area with soap and water, and refrain from using the oil again.

A few of the recipes in this chapter include the optional use of fragrance oils. These are not the same as essential oils, and many fragrance oils sold commercially are synthetic. Be certain any oil you purchase is made from natural ingredients, and if you can only find synthetic fragrance oils, omit them from the recipe.

Finally, women who are pregnant or breastfeeding should consult with their physician and with a professional aromatherapist before using any essential oils. People with medical conditions like diabetes or asthma may also want to check with their physicians. No matter your state of health, always research safety information for every oil you are considering working with.

ESSENTIAL OILS FOR AROMATHERAPEUTIC AND MAGICAL USES

Essential oils are revered for their healing properties, magical energies, and abilities to shift moods and atmospheres with their diverse fragrances. Listed below is a sampling of common essential oils and their uses for both aromatherapy and magic in your self-care routines.

Note that the on-skin uses suggested in "Self-care Application" assume you have diluted the oil(s) in a carrier. (No carrier oil is needed for oil diffusers.)

These brief profiles are followed by recipes featuring blends of essential oils, which include a safe dilution ratio. Again, if you have sensitive skin, allergies, or are pregnant, be extra careful before using essential oils.

BERGAMOT

- **Magical Use:** Bergamot is used for magic that promotes happiness, confidence, success, joy, luck, and peace. It can be used for mental clarity and directing the mind to creative breakthroughs.
- **Aromatherapeutic Use:** Bergamot can be used to soothe skin that has broken out. It can help uplift

moods out of depression, and is best known for the citrus-like fragrance it adds to Earl Grey tea.

- **Self-care Application:** After cleaning your home, use bergamot in an oil diffuser to purify the home and welcome in all of its magical properties. Wear bergamot to get an extra boost of confidence.

CARDAMOM

- **Magical Use:** Cardamom is used for love, sensuality, passion, and lust magic. It can also be used by highly sensitive people to keep energy pure, and by empathetic people to keep energy guarded.

- **Aromatherapeutic Use:** Cardamom has antibacterial properties and is also excellent for relieving nausea and stress.

- **Self-care Application:** Blend three drops rose, cedarwood, and cardamom into coconut oil and use for a romantic massage. In *Magical Aromatherapy*, Scott Cunningham suggests of cardamom: "Visualize love as you smell the intoxicating fragrance. See yourself in an equally beneficial relationship" (p. 68).

CEDARWOOD

- **Magical Use:** Cedarwood is used for purification, healing, spirituality, balance, and grounding magic. When using this oil, you will feel grounded to Earth energy.

- **Aromatherapeutic Use:** Cedarwood is used topically to help with skin problems like acne and eczema. Its fragrance is also soothing and can help calm frazzled nerves.

- **Self-care Application:** Celeste Rayne Heldstab in *Llewellyn's Complete Formulary of Magical Oils* recommends placing 2 or 3 drops each of cypress, juniper, frankincense, sandalwood, and cedarwood oil into an oil diffuser to enhance meditation practices (p. 305).

CHAMOMILE (ROMAN)

- **Magical Use:** Chamomile can be used in success, sleep, meditation, and healing spellwork.
- **Aromatherapeutic Use:** Chamomile can help relieve aches and pains. In a bath, it can soothe PMS and also smooth dry skin. The fragrance can also promote relaxation and assist in getting restful sleep.
- **Self-care Application:** Blend chamomile with geranium for a simple self-healing and self-love blend. Anoint skin with one drop of the blend over any chakra that feels overactive.

CLARY SAGE

- **Magical Use:** Clary sage is used for wisdom, imagination, creativity, and purification magic. Work with this oil to enhance vivid dream imagery and dream recall.
- **Aromatherapeutic Use:** Clary sage relieves tension, PMS, cramps, and anxiety. It can also promote peace of mind, ease headaches, and support better

breathing. Used in skincare, clary sage can help reduce the appearance of wrinkles.

- **Self-care Application:** Blend one drop clary sage and one drop frankincense onto a white candle before doing spiritual and or/ energetic healing.

CYPRESS

- **Magical Use:** Use cypress in healing and purification magic. It is especially helpful in times of change and transition. Cypress can also be used in Otherworldly spells that help guide you through spiritual journeys and vision quests.

- **Aromatherapeutic Use:** Cypress oil is used for relieving painful menstrual cramps and can assist in restoring breath after an asthma attack. It can ease sore muscles and revive circulation when used in massage oil.

- **Self-care Application:** If you are healing after a difficult phase in life or a challenging life event, blend equal parts cypress, marjoram, and geranium oil and use in an oil diffuser or on a warm compress.

EUCALYPTUS

- **Magical Use:** Eucalyptus is used in magic for healing and purification.

- **Aromatherapeutic Use:** Eucalyptus is favored by aromatherapists for its ability to freshen air, and its assistance with healing colds and flus. It is also known as an antibacterial remedy and has been blended into surface cleaners.

- **Self-care Application:** Inhale eucalyptus when you are feeling tense and weak. Use in an oil diffuser with rosemary to purify both the air and energy of a space.

FIR NEEDLE

- **Magical Use:** Use fir needle for refreshing your connection to the earth, and for healing and purification magic.
- **Aromatherapeutic Use:** Fir needle is used to freshen air and can be used for respiratory wellness, especially if you have a cough and/or cold.
- **Self-care Application:** Anoint a green candle with a drop of fir needle and a drop of cedarwood for support in grounding back to the earth.

FRANKINCENSE

- **Magical Use:** Frankincense is used in magic for spirituality and meditation.
- **Aromatherapeutic Use:** Frankincense is celebrated by aromatherapists for relieving tension, anxiety, reducing the appearance of scars and stretch marks, and even helping with breathing problems.
- **Self-care Application:** Use a couple drops of eucalyptus, frankincense, and cedarwood in an oil diffuser while practicing yoga or stretching to promote relaxation and deep breathing. Wear with a drop of vanilla oil to have a deeper love for yourself.

GERANIUM

- **Magical Use:** Geranium is used in magic for happiness, love, and protection.
- **Aromatherapeutic Use:** Geranium essential oil blended with a carrier oil can be used to moisturize skin.
- **Self-care Application:** Blend 3 drops geranium oil, 3 drops grapefruit oil, 3 drops cedarwood oil, 1 tsp. coconut oil, and 1 tsp. aloe. Massage into skin to reduce the appearance of cellulite.

GRAPEFRUIT

- **Magical Use:** Grapefruit can be used for success, happiness, growth, abundance, and pleasure. It is like having the energy of the Nine of Cups in a bottle.
- **Aromatherapeutic Use:** Grapefruit can be used in household cleaners; however, it is also used to relieve muscle aches and tension. It is also said to tone the skin.
- **Self-care Application:** Use a couple drops of grapefruit oil and chamomile oil mixed with a carrier oil to relieve tense and sore muscles. If you want to feel more joy and energy, inhale grapefruit essential oil. Anoint a gold candle with grapefruit oil and a little bit of honey for success magic.

HELICHRYSUM

- **Magical Use:** Helichrysum can be used for dream magic, awakening the imagination, meditation, and success magic. It can be an emotionally supportive oil for sensitive people as well.

- **Aromatherapeutic Use:** Helichrysum is an excellent essential oil for skincare. It also has anti-inflammatory properties, and can ease discomfort from allergies.
- **Self-care Application:** Apply a drop of helichrysum on your chest over your heart if you are a sensitive person who wishes to stay soft and ideal in this harsh world.

JASMINE

- **Magical Use:** Jasmine is used in magic for love and psychic abilities.
- **Aromatherapeutic Use:** Jasmine's dreamy perfume-like scent can soothe stress, help in easing pain from trauma, support self-love, awaken self-confidence, and support emotional wellness.
- **Self-care Application:** Jasmine can help you feel your inner beauty and restore your sense of self-love, especially after trauma. Blend one drop jasmine with one drop vanilla. Anoint on your skin and say the affirmation, *"I am precious, I am magical, I am beautiful, I am valuable."*

LAVENDER

- **Magical Use:** Lavender is used in magic for love, happiness, healing, and peace. According to Scott Cunningham in *Magical Aromatherapy*, "Because it is ruled by Mercury, the planet associated with the conscious mind, lavender's effectiveness in promoting love seems to lie in its ability to change the way we think about love" (p. 102).

- **Aromatherapeutic Use:** Lavender can be used to assist in breathing deeply as well as to promote relaxation and calmness.

- **Self-care Application:** To soothe and calm an overactive mind or aid in healing after anxiety or a panic attack, dampen a washcloth and put a drop each of helichrysum, frankincense, and lavender into the cloth. Place on your forehead and rest easy.

LEMON

- **Magical Use:** Lemon is used in magic for healing and purification.

- **Aromatherapeutic Use:** Lemon can help sanitize surfaces as a cleaner. However, it can also be gently inhaled as a decongestant.

- **Self-care Application:** Blend a couple drops each of lemon, eucalyptus, and rosemary oil and rub on your chest if you have a stuffy nose.

LEMONGRASS

- **Magical Use:** Lemongrass is used in magic for healing and psychic abilities.

- **Aromatherapeutic Use:** Lemongrass can work as a natural insect repellant and air deodorizer. It can also be used to soothe sore muscles.

- **Self-care Application:** Anoint a piece of citrine with lemongrass oil and carry when you are participating in artistic endeavors, and/or when you wish to easily download your next creation.

MARJORAM

- **Magical Use:** Marjoram is used in peace, healing, and restorative magic.
- **Aromatherapeutic Use:** Marjoram has antibacterial and antiviral properties, making it an excellent essential oil to have on hand if you are suffering from a cold or the flu.
- **Self-care Application:** Blend marjoram, cypress, and frankincense to help during difficult transitions and wear to assist with moving through grief.

NEROLI

- **Magical Use:** Neroli is used in magic for purification and relief. It is an essential oil of manifestation. It is also said to conjure courage, inner strength, and wisdom.
- **Aromatherapeutic Use:** Neroli is used in skincare for rejuvenating mature skin. It is a calming fragrance and can help relax heightened moods. Its fragrance is popular in perfume and blends very nicely with jasmine.
- **Self-care Application:** According to Margaret Ann Lembo in *The Essential Guide to Aromatherapy and Vibrational Healing*, Neroli can help bring back memories from Atlantis (p. 198). If you are doing some soul searching and wish to connect with ancient wisdom of Atlantis, anoint a blue candle with neroli oil.

Surround the candle with aquamarine, ocean jasper, emerald, and/or Atlantisite crystals.

PATCHOULI

- **Magical Use:** Patchouli is used in magic for love, lust, prosperity and attraction. Anoint patchouli on a tonka bean and carry in your wallet or purse to attract money and love into your life. While it is connected to earthly delights, patchouli can also be incorporated into spiritual blends.

- **Aromatherapeutic Use:** Patchouli's earthy fragrance can relieve and soothe stress. Used topically, patchouli can relieve dry skin and scrapes.

- **Self-care Application:** Use a drop of patchouli with a drop of tea tree oil on acne breakouts. Add a few drops to a relaxing bath.

PEPPERMINT

- **Magical Use:** Peppermint is used in magic for mental agility, purification, breakthroughs, and optimism.

- **Aromatherapeutic Use:** Peppermint offers excellent breathing support for those with asthma and colds. It can also relieve tension headaches. Peppermint is now a very popular digestive supplement for those suffering from IBS.

- **Self-care Application:** Add a couple drops each of peppermint and lemon to an oil diffuser to purify your home and draw in vibrant and happy energies.

ROSE

- **Magical Use:** Rose is used in magic for love, beauty, pleasure, peace, and healing.

- **Aromatherapeutic Use:** Rose is a powerful ingredient in skincare, helping to make skin glow and reduce signs of aging.

- **Self-care Application:** Blend equal parts rose, patchouli, and frankincense oils for a deeply pleasant experience. Wear or inhale to facilitate a loving sense of self and explore your deepest desires.

ROSEMARY

- **Magical Use:** Rosemary is used for mental agility and purification. It is also believed to be a protective oil.

- **Aromatherapeutic Use:** Rosemary oil can help relieve aches and is often an added ingredient in shampoos for dandruff and/or hair loss. When inhaled, rosemary has revitalizing powers, awakening the mind and spirit to focus and take action.

- **Self-care Application:** Add one drop rosemary and one drop patchouli to your conditioner to soothe your scalp (the conditioner will act as the carrier). Diffuse rosemary oil when you are studying and need to retain a lot of information.

SANDALWOOD

- **Magical Use:** Sandalwood is used for psychic abilities, spirituality, and meditation.

- **Aromatherapeutic Use:** Sandalwood is mostly known for its energetic abilities. However, it is also used topically for skincare and to help with sore throats and colds.
- **Self-care Application:** Sandalwood on its own is wonderful to wear for meditation. Diffuse or wear sandalwood with frankincense and lavender to experience deep wisdom and spiritual discovery.

SWEET ORANGE

- **Magical Use:** Orange is used in magic for happiness and positive energy as it eradicates negative thinking and lower-frequency energies. It can assist in success and manifestation magic as well, offering the power of the sun to promote growth in spells.
- **Aromatherapeutic Use:** Sweet orange can brighten moods and is especially useful if you suffer from Seasonal Affective Disorder. Since it has antibacterial and antiseptic properties, sweet orange makes an excellent addition to home cleaning products.
- **Self-care Application:** Anoint a piece of carnelian with one drop sweet orange and one drop grapefruit oil. Hold the carnelian in your hands and inhale the citrus fragrance, saying the following affirmation: *"I am optimistic, I am hopeful, I am confident, I am successful."* Carry this carnelian in your pocket on days you need a boost of confidence.

TEA TREE

- **Magical Use:** Tea tree can be used in healing and purification magic.

- **Aromatherapeutic Use:** Tea tree oil is revered for its antibacterial abilities and is a staple in health food stores. It's often used on skin to relieve acne, or even on gums to prevent gingivitis.

- **Self-care Application:** Mix 2 tbsp. unrefined virgin coconut oil with two drops tea tree and two drops peppermint oil for a mouth rinse.

THYME

- **Magical Use:** Thyme can be used for intellectual prowess, courage, and healing magic.

- **Aromatherapeutic Use:** Thyme can be used as a decongestant when inhaled. Thyme is also revered for its antibacterial properties.

- **Self-care Application:** Anoint the corners of a mirror that you use daily with a couple drops of thyme oil. Every time you look in the mirror, know that it will help you find courage to explore your potential and passions.

VANILLA

- **Magical Use:** Use vanilla in love, beauty, sensuality, and attraction spell work.

- **Aromatherapeutic Use:** Vanilla oil may have aphrodisiac properties. It can also be used to support respiratory health. It can be used in skincare to reduce signs of aging.

- **Self-care Application:** A blissful blend to wear or diffuse is equal parts vanilla, sweet orange, and jasmine. Wear when you need a little support feeling the best about yourself.

VETIVER

- **Magical Use:** Vetiver is used for abundance, grounding, balance, and self-esteem.
- **Aromatherapeutic Use:** Vetiver can be used to relieve tension and insomnia. It can lower anxiety, and is a good support oil for those in recovery.
- **Self-care Application:** Diffuse vetiver, cedarwood, and patchouli oil for a woodsy, grounding experience.

YLANG YLANG

- **Magical Use:** Ylang ylang is used in magic for love, sexuality, and peace.
- **Aromatherapeutic Use:** Ylang ylang is a very sweet and strong floral fragrance, and has powerful sedative properties that can induce euphoria. It is also used to help with high blood pressure as well as depression.
- **Self-care Application:** Wear or diffuse ylang ylang with vanilla and orange when you are feeling low in spirits, or need to shake off stagnant energy.

HANDS-ON BEAUTY: MAGICAL SELF-CARE CREATIONS

Create your own self-care spa experience with these natural, magically-enhanced spellcrafts. Essential oils are useful for a wide variety of applications, from face masks to cleaning products, all while adding a touch of Aromatherapy to the experience. Keep in mind, however, that no matter the ingredients, the magical component of any working is always you.

As you follow these recipes, be sure to visualize your intended outcome for the finished product. When finished, charge the container by holding it in your hands and sending your energy into it. If you like, you can create your own incantations to incorporate into the process.

PURIFYING FACE MASK

This is a homemade face mask for beauty that you can make with essential oils and ingredients from the kitchen. The ingredients will help purify and balance your skin, leaving you with a bright glow. In this recipe, the aloe and honey act as the carrier for the essential oils.

You will need:

- 2 tbsp. banana, mashed
- 1 tbsp. aloe vera gel
- ½ tsp. raw honey
- 1 drop chamomile
- 1 drop lemongrass
- 1 drop ylang ylang

Instructions:

Mix all of the ingredients in a small bowl, visualizing your skin feeling cleansed and refreshed.

Apply evenly to clean and dry skin. Leave on for 10 to 15 minutes and rinse off well.

FACE SERUM FOR BEAUTY

This recipe is meant to give your skin a youthful, refreshing glow while keeping it balanced and healthy. The optional blue tansy oil is particularly great for balancing skin and reducing signs of aging.

You will need:

- 4-dram glass vial
- 1 ½ tsp. rose hip carrier oil
- 1 ½ tsp. jojoba carrier oil
- 1 drop helichrysum
- 1 drop frankincense
- 1 drop sandalwood
- 1 drop geranium
- 1 drop rose
- 1 drop blue tansy oil (optional)

Instructions:

Add the essential oils into a 4-dram glass vial.

Slowly add equal amounts of rose hip and jojoba carrier oils and blend, visualizing the cells of your skin absorbing all the nutrients they need for healing and restoration.

Wash your face as you normally do.

Gently apply a very small amount to your face, being careful to avoid getting too close to your eyes. Gently dab your skin with your fingertips until the serum has been absorbed.

COFFEE AND SUGAR SCRUB FOR LOVE

This is a soothing and invigorating scrub that you can use to welcome love and lust into your life—it would be great to use before a date! The coconut oil will make your skin feel soft and moisturized while the coffee will help with circulation.

You will need:

- 1 cup sugar
- ½ cup coconut oil
- 2 tbsp. ground coffee
- 9 drops vanilla
- 6 drops patchouli
- 3 drops rose
- 3 drops cardamom

Instructions:

Blend the sugar and the coconut oil together. Stir in the coffee.

Slowly stir in the essential oils, adding slowly in case you wish to modify the scent. Visualize your skin becoming energized, sensual, and vibrant as you blend in the oils.

PEACHES AND CREAM SWEET TALK LIP SCRUB

This is a lip scrub that you can easily make at home and preserve in a small container. Use it when you need to remember to "speak sweetly" through the day. In other words, use this to help you keep your words about yourself and the world around you in a space of optimism and hope.

You will need:

- 1 tbsp. coconut oil (extra virgin, unrefined, organic)
- 1 tbsp. raw fine sugar
- 2-3 drops vanilla food grade flavoring
- 2-3 drops peach food grade flavoring

Instructions:

Mix all the ingredients together in a small bowl until well blended.

Hold the bowl in your hands and envision it glowing with bright orange, yellow, gold, and pink light.

Say the following incantation:

"From my lips to the world and to myself: I speak kindly, sweetly, and with love."

Place in small container.

Gently rub into your lips with your fingers, and then rinse. You can repeat the incantation whenever you use the scrub.

BATH SALTS TO RELIEVE PMS

This soothing combination of essential oils and salts will help to ease muscle tension as well as relieve anxiety and hormonal imbalances brought on due to PMS. Pour into hot bath water and enjoy the feeling of muscle aches melting away.

<u>You will need</u>:

- 2 cups Epsom salt
- 1 tbsp. coconut oil
- 4 drops rose
- 3 drops geranium
- 4 drops chamomile
- 4 drops lavender
- 3 drops clary sage
- 3 drops marjoram

<u>Instructions</u>:

If the coconut oil is solid, place it in a mug or small bowl, then place that in a larger heat-safe bowl of hot water until melted.

Blend the Epsom salt and the coconut oil together.

Slowly stir in the essential oils, adding slowly in case you wish to modify the scent. Visualize the restorative powers of the oils enveloping you with soothing, healing energies.

WHITE LIGHT SPRAY

This is a spray to release into the air when you feel like your area needs extra purification. It reinforces the protective energies around you. Use in your car, in your home after an argument, or simply when you want to refresh your energy.

<u>You will need</u>:

- 4 oz spray bottle
- 10-11 tbsp. distilled water
- 1 ½ tbsp. rubbing alcohol

- 45 drops clary sage
- 30 drops frankincense
- 25 drops cedarwood
- 20 drops neroli
- 20 drops fir needle
- 10 drops rosemary
- 1 tsp dried hyssop flower
- Sprig of rosemary
- 1 tsp dried garden sage leaf
- Smoky quartz crystal chips

Instructions:

Using a funnel, slowly add the rubbing alcohol into the bottle.

Add in the crystals, followed by the dried herbs.

Add in the essential oils.

Top off with the distilled water—you will likely use between 10 tbsp and 11 tbsp.

Hold the bottle in your hands and visualize the contents becoming saturated with white, purifying light.

ANTIBACTERIAL CLEANING SPRAY FOR HEALING AND PURIFICATION

This is a spray that you can use to clean surfaces. Not only do the essential oils have antibacterial and antiviral properties that clean and sanitize, but they are also used magically for their healing and purifying properties as well.

You will need:

- 4 oz spray bottle

- 8 tbsp. rubbing alcohol
- 4 tbsp. aloe vera gel
- 35 drops grapefruit
- 30 drops lemon
- 30 drops lemongrass
- 30 drops tea tree
- 15 drops rosemary
- 10 drops thyme

Instructions:

Using a funnel, pour the rubbing alcohol into the bottle. Add the essential oils, then top off with the aloe vera gel.

Close the bottle and shake vigorously to mix the contents, while visualizing all surfaces in your home becoming clean and sparkling.

ABUNDANCE HAND CREAM

This decadent lotion takes a little extra effort to make, but it's an effective moisturizer for your hands, and the essential oils will help draw money into your life.

NOTE: Bergamot oil is photosensitive, meaning it can cause burns when exposed to sunlight. If you use this hand cream, avoid exposure to direct sunlight on the applied area for 12 to 48 hours, depending on the dilution ratio and your personal sensitivity.

You will need:

- ½ cup sweet almond oil
- ¼ cup coconut oil
- 1 tbsp. plus 1 tsp. beeswax
- 1 tbsp. plus 1 tsp. shea butter
- ½ cup aloe vera gel
- 4 drops patchouli

- 4 drops vetiver
- 4 drops cedarwood
- 4 drops bergamot
- 4 drops honeysuckle fragrance oil (optional)

Instructions:

Put a mixing bowl into a double boiler and slowly melt the almond oil, coconut oil, beeswax, and shea butter until well blended. If you don't have a double boiler, you can place the mixing bowl inside a larger, heat-proof bowl with hot water in it. (If the water cools before the mixture melts, replace it with more hot water.)

Remove from heat and let cool for about 30 minutes.

Stir in the essential oils. Put the bowl in the refrigerator to continue cooling for an hour.

Using a hand mixer, blend the cooled ingredients, slowly adding in the aloe vera gel.

Every time you use this lotion, envision yourself holding thick wads of cash, running your hands through a large bowl of gold and silver coins, or whatever tactile image makes you feel abundant.

EARTHING FOOT SCRUB

This exfoliating salt scrub will make your feet nice and smooth. The essential oils will help you feel grounded and connected to Gaia energy.

You will need:

- 1 cup coarse sea salt
- 2 – 4 tbsp. jojoba carrier oil
- 5 drops cedarwood
- 5 drops patchouli

- 5 drops vetiver
- 5 drops cypress
- 3 drops fir needle

Instructions:

Pour the sea salt into a mixing bowl.

Slowly add in the carrier oil—use just enough to make the sea salt feel slightly damp. You do not want the scrub to be too dry or too oily.

Add in the essential oils and stir to blend well.

Use the scrub on your legs and feet while envisioning yourself standing in a natural outdoor setting, with your feet planted firmly on the ground, absorbing Earth's energy.

Note: be sure not to use it right after you've shaved!

SOOTHING MILK AND HONEY BATH

The ingredients of this soothing bath will enhance your sense of self-love and appreciation. It is a comforting and relaxing soak that will also help you discover your unique brand of beauty and enchantment.

You will need:

- 2 cups whole milk
- 2 tbs. honey
- 5 drops rose oil
- 5 drops vanilla oil
- 5 drops lavender oil
- 5 drops jasmine oil

Instructions:

Fill the bath at a comfortable warm temperature. Add the ingredients, and stir well with your hand to ensure an even dispersal of the milk, honey, and oils before getting into the tub.

To enhance this self-care experience, light pink and white candles and pour a glass of rosé or hibiscus tea to enjoy!

ESSENTIAL OIL BLENDS FOR MAGICAL SELF-CARE

The following blend recipes address a variety of self-care needs. They are formulated for use on skin, but remember to do a patch test of any new blend first. Choose a carrier oil on the lighter side, such as sweet almond, apricot kernel, or avocado oil—feel free to experiment, or just use what you have on hand.

These blends can also be used in an oil diffuser. However, most diffusers are not meant for carrier oils, and it's not recommended to use carrier oils in diffuser blends. If you'd like the option to use the recipes below in a diffuser, simply omit the carrier oil from the recipe and use a 2-dram bottle in place of the 4-oz bottle, to minimize oxidation of the oils.

You can then create a skin-safe version as-needed, by diluting a few drops of the blend in a teaspoon or two of carrier oil (or more, if the blend is particularly potent). Be sure to take this step before trying any of the suggested uses below!

Whichever approach you take, remember to focus on your intentions for the finished blend as you work. Hold a vision in your mind that represents how you want to feel when using the oil.

TENSION AND HEADACHE OIL BLEND

This is an aromatherapeutic blend for when you are feeling tension in your body. It will also assist in relieving headaches—just put a small drop on your temples and the back of your neck. You can also rub a couple drops into a damp cloth and lay it over your forehead.

NOTE: Bergamot oil is photosensitive, meaning it can cause burns when exposed to sunlight. If you use this blend, avoid exposure to direct sunlight on the applied area for 12 to 48 hours, depending on the dilution ratio and your personal sensitivity.

You will need:

- 4-oz glass bottle
- 10 drops lavender
- 10 drops rosemary
- 8 drops bergamot
- 7 drops peppermint
- 6 drops eucalyptus
- 6 drops clary sage
- Carrier oil to top off the blend (fractionated coconut or sweet almond are good choices for this recipe)

Instructions:

Slowly add the essential oils into the glass bottle.

Fill to the top with the carrier oil.

Shake well to blend.

DEEP BREATH OIL BLEND

This oil blend is meant to support strong breathing, breathwork exercises, and engaging in deeper breaths. Put into an oil diffuser or use a couple drops on a washcloth while in the shower. You can also apply this blend to your chest before going to bed to help with breathing while you sleep.

You will need:

- 4-oz glass bottle
- 5 drops eucalyptus
- 5 drops peppermint
- 3 drops rosemary
- 3 drops fir needle
- 2 drops tea tree
- 2 drops cardamom
- 2 drops lavender
- 2 drops frankincense
- Carrier oil to top off the blend (fractionated coconut or sweet almond are good choices for this recipe)

Instructions:

Slowly add the essential oils the glass bottle.

Fill to the top with the carrier oil.

Shake well to blend.

HEART HEALING OIL BLEND

This blend can be used to support processing the grief of loss and sorrow of heartbreak. If you are feeling sadness from loss, use this blend in an oil diffuser or wear a couple drops on your heart chakra.

NOTE: Bergamot oil is photosensitive, meaning it can cause burns when exposed to sunlight. If you use this blend, avoid exposure to direct sunlight on the applied area for 12 to 48 hours, depending on the dilution ratio and your personal sensitivity.

You will need:

- 4-oz glass bottle
- 6 drops marjoram
- 7 drops geranium
- 6 drops helichrysum
- 3 drops chamomile
- 7 drops bergamot
- 3 drops vanilla
- 5 drops heliotrope fragrance oil (optional)
- Carrier oil to top off the blend

Instructions:

Slowly add the essential oils into the glass bottle.

Fill to the top with the carrier oil.

Shake well to blend.

WISE STUDENT OIL BLEND

Use this blend when you need to conjure intense focus and concentration. You can wear this or use in an oil diffuser. For a stronger magical enhancement, anoint a yellow candle with this oil. Burn the candle when you are studying.

NOTE: Bergamot and lemon oils are photosensitive, meaning they can cause burns when exposed to sunlight. If you use this blend, avoid exposure to direct sunlight on the applied area for 12 to 48 hours, depending on the dilution ratio and your personal sensitivity.

You will need:

- 4-oz glass bottle
- 5 drops bergamot
- 5 drops sweet orange
- 5 drops lemon
- 3 drops rosemary
- 2 drops ylang ylang
- 1 drop almond fragrance oil (optional)
- Carrier oil to top off the blend. Sweet almond oil is recommended for this blend as almond is associated intellectual prowess.

Instructions:

Slowly add the essential oils into the glass bottle.

Fill to the top with the carrier oil, if using on skin.

Shake well to blend.

FRIENDSHIP OIL BLEND

This oil blend can help you feel joy, happiness, and bliss, all while attracting new friends and feeling gratitude for the friends you already have. Wear this blend in new social situations or when you need a little support with being social and friendly. If you're making a diffuser blend, omit the herbs (and carrier oil).

NOTE: Bergamot and lemon oils are photosensitive, meaning they can cause burns when exposed to sunlight. If you use this blend, avoid exposure to direct sunlight on the applied area for 12 to 48 hours, depending on the dilution ratio and your personal sensitivity.

You will need:

- 4-oz glass bottle
- 9 drops bergamot
- 9 drops lemon
- 9 drops lavender
- 9 drops vanilla
- 2 dried sweet pea blossoms
- 2 dried apple seeds
- Small pinch of dried catnip
- Carrier oil to top off the blend

Instructions:

Slowly add the essential oils into the glass bottle.

Add the herbs and seeds.

Add the essential oils.

Fill to the top with a carrier oil.

Shake well to blend.

SPIRITUAL AWAKENING OIL BLEND

This oil blend will conjure psychic abilities and is excellent to wear or use in an oil diffuser when you are meditating or doing magical work. Anoint a purple candle with this blend or anoint a piece of lapis lazuli and carry with you when you are wishing to feel spiritual wisdom.

If you would like to make this a perfume that you wear daily, consider adding fragrance oils to it. Slowly incorporate coconut, heliotrope, and gardenia fragrances (one or two drops at a time) to give this oil a very tropical and inviting fragrance.

You will need:

- 4-oz glass bottle
- 8 drops sandalwood
- 6 drops frankincense
- 6 drops neroli
- 3 drops lemongrass
- 3 drops jasmine
- Coconut, heliotrope, and gardenia fragrance oils (optional)
- Carrier oil to top off the blend (fractionated coconut or sweet almond are good choices for this recipe)

Instructions:

Slowly add the essential oils into the glass bottle.

Add fragrance oils (if using).

Fill to the top with the carrier oil.

Shake well to blend.

Chapter Five: BOTANICAL MAGIC: SELF-CARE FOR THE GREEN WITCH

The act of working with plants is arguably a form of self-care in and of itself. Many a gardener has stepped into the garden with the intention to just take care of one quick task, and wound up spending an hour or more doing far more than they planned, simply because it feels so good to be there.

Likewise, many people have noticed that simply watering or pruning their indoor plants has a calming or even uplifting effect on their energy. Those who grow their own culinary herbs will swear that nothing tastes better in a meal than herbs they've just snipped from a pot on the window sill.

Our bodies inherently resonate with the energies of the natural world. This is why they respond favorably to working with crystals and essential oils, and to the healthy, fresh foods we nourish them with. Our spirits also need connection with nature.

Nothing can quite compare to how we feel after a hike in the woods, a swim in a lake, or a peaceful night spent sleeping under the stars. Sometimes, these activities provide the most potent magic we can experience in our human bodies—no candles, charms, or incantations required.

Witches, especially those on a green path, take this inherent connection to nature a step further, by working with the magical energies of the plant world. Whether we're full-fledged gardeners or we simply keep an indoor plant or two, we utilize both the physical and metaphysical benefits of herbs, flowers, and other plant life as part of our practice.

In this chapter, we'll examine some of the most valuable herbs, plants, and flowers for witches in light of their benefits to our physical, emotional, and spiritual well-being. Most are readily available as potted plants for growing, and/or in dried form for magical workings. (And if you don't already tend plants of your own, hopefully this chapter will inspire you to consider at least bringing a potted plant or two into your home.

BASIL

- **Holistic Uses:** Basil is a common and delicious herb used to flavor a variety of dishes. Basil supports a healthy digestion and has anti-inflammatory properties.
- **Magical Uses:** Basil is truly a catch-all herb for a variety of magic, as it can be used for prosperity, love, luck, protection, and banishment spellwork. It has a friendly, yet powerful energy—a little can go a long way! Cook up a comforting self-love pasta dinner for yourself with tomato, garlic, and basil. Keep a $2 bill in a small bag with dried basil and patchouli to attract good fortune.

BEE BALM

- **Holistic Uses:** Bee balm tea was used by Native American tribes to help relieve colds, headaches, fevers, and sore throats. It is also an excellent tea to ease stomach indigestion.

- **Magical Uses:** Bee balm can be used in abundance spells, meditation, love, and friendship spells. Add bee balm buds to prosperity sachets and honey jars to attract abundance. Carry bee balm to attract friends.

CALENDULA

- **Holistic Uses:** Calendula petals are revered for their ability to heal skin. In a salve, calendula can soothe eczema and rashes.

- **Magical Uses:** Calendula is used in divination and psychic spell work. It is also said to protect against negativity through radiating positivity and embodying the strength and power of the sun. Brew a tea made with ½ tsp. calendula, ½ tsp. mugwort, and ½ bee balm and drink before doing divination. Plant calendula in the front of your home to welcome in positive energy. In his *Encyclopedia of Magical Herbs*, Scott Cunningham suggests "Marigolds, picked at noon when the sun is at its hottest and strongest, will strengthen and comfort the heart" (p.149).

CATNIP

- **Holistic Uses:** Catnip has relaxing properties. It has been used in teas to assist in relaxation and helping the body to rest and sleep better.

- **Magical Uses:** Catnip can be used for love, beauty, and friendship magic. It will bring joy to an environment, radiating mellow, yet powerful, happy energy. In *The Modern Witchcraft Guide to Magical Herbs*, Judy Ann Nock suggests, "When faced with a particularly difficult challenge, drinking an infusion of catnip or wearing a sprig either fresh or dried in a charm will make obstacles easier to overcome" (p.140).

CHAMOMILE

- **Holistic Uses:** Chamomile has a sedative quality to it, helping to foster a restful mind, quality sleep, and calmness. It can calm digestive issues as well as nerves.

- **Magical Uses:** Chamomile is used in magic for peace, success, abundance, love, and purification. Have a simple cup of chamomile tea at the end of the day. Hold the mug of tea and say the following: *"A productive day leads to a restful eve. I find peace and comfort with this cup of tea."*

DAISY

- **Holistic Uses:** While daisies may not be a go-to for holistic healing, the flowers are said to have anti-inflammatory properties.

- **Magical Uses:** Daisies can be used in magic for happiness, love, fertility, good health, and friendship. Keep a bouquet of fresh daisies in your home to keep the energy of the house happy and content.

DANDELION

- **Holistic Uses:** Dandelion tea is said to help cleanse the liver and act as a diuretic, supporting the bladder and kidneys. The leaves, flowers, and roots are all edible.
- **Magical Uses:** Dandelion is used for wishes, abundance, and psychic magic. Drink a tea made of dandelion leaves and mugwort to have vivid and prophetic dreams.

ECHINACEA

- **Holistic Uses:** Echinacea is well-known as an herb that can support the immune system.
- **Magical Uses:** Echinacea is used for youthfulness, speedy healing, fertility, and love magic. Grow echinacea in your garden to ensure health for all of those who reside in your home.

FENNEL

- **Holistic Uses:** Fennel seeds can help aid digestive discomfort.
- **Magical Uses:** Fennel can be used in magic for healing, attracting friends, and protection against evil. Carry fennel seeds to attract friendly people while keeping away unpleasant personalities.

HIBISCUS

- **Holistic Uses:** Hibiscus has a good amount of vitamin C and adds a bright citrus note and lovely color to a cup of tea.
- **Magical Uses:** Hibiscus flowers are excellent for love magic and honoring the heart chakra. Use dried hibiscus flowers in love potions.

HONEYSUCKLE

- **Holistic Uses:** While honeysuckle isn't commonly thought of as a holistic remedy, the flowers are said to be anti-inflammatory. As a Bach flower remedy, it is used to relieve homesickness and assist those who feel like they're living in the past.
- **Magical Uses:** Honeysuckle is used for spirituality, psychic abilities, love, and abundance magic. Tie together a sprig of honeysuckle and a vanilla bean to sweeten your luck and blessings.

HYSSOP

- **Holistic Uses:** Hyssop is used to relieve breathing issues and can be added to teas and lozenges to relieve coughs and asthma.
- **Magical Uses:** Hyssop is used for protection and purification. Add hyssop blossoms to herbal smoke wands or hang hyssop around your home to keep boundaries up and negativity out.

LAVENDER

- **Holistic Uses:** Lavender is known to be an incredible calming agent, and can be very soothing when added to a tea. In an herbal wash it can be soothing to the skin and support the clearing of fungal infections.
- **Magical Uses:** Lavender can assist in spiritual work and meditation. It is also used for love and healing magic. If you are feeling self-doubt or having critical thoughts, hold lavender flowers to return to a state of peace and love.

LEMON BALM

- **Holistic Uses:** Lemon balm is a soothing herb with a comforting lemon fragrance. It can be used to help ease anxiety and soothe indigestion. It is used to uplift moods and can support those suffering from Seasonal Affective Disorder (SAD).
- **Magical Uses:** Lemon balm is used to attract friendship, happiness, and love. Blend fresh lemon balm leaves and honey in a tea to sweeten your mood.

MEADOWSWEET

- **Holistic Uses:** Meadowsweet can be a supportive herb for those with ulcers, IBS, heartburn or digestive irritation.
- **Magical Uses:** Meadowsweet can be used in magic for healing and happiness. It is also connected to psychic abilities and considered to be a Fae-friendly herb, inviting in nature spirits. Keep a purple bag of

meadowsweet, vervain, mugwort, and peppermint with your divination tools to keep their energy vibrant.

MUGWORT

- **Holistic Uses:** Mugwort is used in traditional Chinese medicine as a liver tonic and also in some acupuncture treatments.

- **Magical Uses:** Mugwort can be used to enhance psychic abilities and to support divination work. Any spell that involves dreams, divination, or improving intuition would benefit from mugwort. Make a mugwort tea rinse, then wash divination tools (such as runes or a pendulum) with it.

MULLEIN

- **Holistic Uses:** Mullein is an expectorant and can be used to help clear coughs and colds.

- **Magical Uses:** Mullein is used in healing spells and can also restore peace and balance to situations. In some Northern European witchcraft traditions, stalks of dried mullein were covered in wax and lit as candles, which are known as "Hag's Tapers." When you are embarking on a spiritual journey, place mullein blossoms in a vase surrounded with mookaite jasper and white candles.

NASTURTIUM

- **Holistic Uses:** Nasturtium is an edible flower with a mildly peppery taste that is a pretty addition to salads.

- **Magical Uses:** Nasturtium can be used for empowerment, spirituality, and purification magic. Carry nasturtium blossoms with carnelian when you need to have courage.

PEPPERMINT

- **Holistic Uses:** Peppermint can be very soothing for indigestion. Along with rosemary, it can help jumpstart a sluggish mental state.
- **Magical Uses:** Peppermint can be used for attracting love, abundance, and good health into your life. Blend peppermint leaves into a healing smoothie to help keep your gut happy.

RED CLOVER

- **Holistic Uses:** Red clover is an excellent ingredient to add to tea blends for respiratory issues. A tincture can be added topically to help with skin issues. The red flower itself is edible, highly nutritious, and a nice garnish on a salad.
- **Magical Uses:** Red clover is used in purification and protection magic. Carry a red clover with you to protect your energy from toxic people.

ROSE

- **Holistic Uses:** Rose water is purifying for the skin.
- **Magical Uses:** The rose is a powerful flower used in love, peace, beauty, sensuality, and attraction magic. The stems and thorns of roses can be used in

protection magic. Keep fresh roses on your altar to attract love into your life while keeping you safe from harmful energies. Use rose petals in baths to surround yourself with a deep, luxurious sense of beauty.

ROSEMARY

- **Holistic Uses:** Rosemary can help restore memory. Rosemary tea can be used as a hair rinse to support hair and scalp health.

- **Magical Uses:** Rosemary can be used in purification and protection magic. It can also be used to enhance mental prowess. Dried rosemary can be burned as a simple purification incense. Keep rosemary by your desk where you study or work.

RUE

- **Holistic Uses:** Rue has been used as a poultice directly on the skin to reduce swelling from sprains. It is also an ingredient in Four Thieves Vinegar.

- **Magical Uses:** Rue is a protective herb that wards off worry, negativity, and harmful thinking. It can be used to assist in creativity as well. Wrap a sprig of rue with a sprig of rosemary and keep it close by if you are feeling overwhelmed by worry or overly critical thoughts.

SAGE

- **Holistic Uses:** A sage tea can be used to rinse out the mouth as a mouthwash.

- **Magical Uses:** Sage from the garden can be used as a purifying and protective incense in place of white sage. It can assist in promoting wise and spiritual thinking as well as enhance prosperity spells. Create a simmering potpourri on your stovetop using sage, rosemary, tulsi, and thyme to awaken your mind and purify the energy of your house. Put two cups of water into a saucepan on your stove and keep it on a low setting. Add 1 tsp of each dried herb.

ST. JOHN'S WORT

- **Holistic Uses:** St. John's Wort is well known as a supplemental treatment for depression and stress.
- **Magical Uses:** St. John's Wort can be used to attract happiness and abundance, and protect from negativity and bad attitudes. Incorporate into potions and teas for joy. Carry with sweet pea flowers to attract good times with friends.

SUNFLOWER

- **Holistic Uses:** Sunflowers are edible plants, with the seeds being a favorite easy snack full of nutrients.
- **Magical Uses:** Sunflowers can be used in empowerment and courage magic. They can also assist in magic meant to conjure joy, positivity, and good luck. Give a sunflower bouquet to a friend to show gratitude and love. Use sunflower petals in oil blends or sachets to conjure the power of the sun.

SWEET PEA

- **Holistic Uses:** Sweet pea isn't necessarily used as a holistic remedy. However, the flower essence of sweet pea is said to assist with trust, finding comfort, and cultivating gentleness and tenderness.

- **Magical Uses:** Sweet pea can attract friends and benevolent nature spirits. Grow sweet pea in your garden to welcome friendship and domestic comfort to your home.

THYME

- **Holistic Uses:** Thyme is said to help relieve headaches. A tea of thyme can be used as a mouthwash.

- **Magical Uses:** Thyme is used in magic for love, purification, and courage. In *Herb Magic*, Patti Wigington suggests: "If you are facing a challenge, brew the leaves into an infusion and, once it cools, dab a bit on your pulse points to help you conquer your fears and give you courage under pressure" (p.111).

TULSI

- **Holistic Uses:** Tulsi, also known as holy basil, is a revered herb celebrated for its powers to warm and heal the heart. It has a calming effect on the body when taken internally. It is also said to have antibiotic and antibacterial properties.

- **Magical Uses:** Tulsi is said to be the embodiment of the Hindu goddess Lakshmi, who is the goddess of abundance and love. While it is an herb closely aligned to the heart, it can balance all the chakras. Drink a tea of tulsi, ginger, and mint if you are starting to feel a bit under the weather.

VERVAIN

- **Holistic Uses:** Also known as verbena, vervain is said to have anti-inflammatory properties and is useful in relieving headaches and muscle pain. It has a sedative effect as a tea.
- **Magical Uses:** Vervain is used for love spells, spirituality, and purification. Keep vervain and yarrow together to assist with loving spiritual growth.

VIOLET

- **Holistic Uses:** Violet has been used topically to treat a variety of skin conditions, from dry skin to insect bites. Rich in vitamins A and C, fresh violets also make for lovely decorative edibles in a variety of dishes.
- **Magical Uses:** Violets can be used in spells for love and friendship. Drink a tea of violet, rose, tulsi, and sage to help reveal your soul's purpose, your life's passion, and the path you wish to take next.

YARROW

- **Holistic Uses:** Yarrow is an excellent support herb when trying to reduce a fever, relax muscle tension, or relieve menstrual cramps.
- **Magical Uses:** Yarrow is used for magical enhancement, psychic abilities, and love spells. Drink a

tea of yarrow, rose, and mugwort before bed to dream of your magical powers and soul's purpose.

GARDENS FOR SELF-CARE

If you're lucky enough to already have a garden, or have access to space where you can start one, you can plant flowers and herbs that generate special and specific energies. Many of these plants are also suitable for container gardens, so all you really need is a balcony or an indoor area with sufficient sunlight.

- **To attract friends:** Bee balm, catnip, daffodils, daisies, fennel, lemon balm, sunflower, sweet pea, yellow roses
- **To attract abundance and prosperity:** Basil, beans, cabbage, chamomile, dill, honeysuckle, kale, mints, pumpkin, spinach, wild bergamot
- **To attract love and sensuality:** Bleeding heart, catnip, dill, hibiscus, lavender, marjoram, rose, strawberries, vervain, violets, yarrow
- **To generate peaceful and healing energies:** Chamomile, cucumber, echinacea, hops, lavender, lemon balm, lemongrass, meadowsweet, marjoram, St. John's wort, thyme, vervain
- **To generate happiness and joy:** Calendula, catnip, daisies, daffodils, irises, sunflowers, St. John's Wort, tulips

- **To access psychic abilities and spiritual wisdom:** Blue salvia, calendula, mugwort, parsley, sage, rosemary, tulsi, vervain, wormwood, yarrow
- **To create a protective boundary:** Basil, fennel, garlic, hyssop, peppers, rosemary, rue, sage, thyme
- **To celebrate the moon:** Begonias, cosmos, evening primrose, gardenia, hydrangea, lemon balm, melons, moonflower, mugwort, poppies, yarrow
- **To welcome nature spirits and the Fae:** Bee balm, berries, bluebells, columbine, foxglove, honeysuckle, meadowsweet, morning glory, St. John's Wort, sweet pea, thyme, violets

INDOOR PLANT POWER

Whether or not you're able to maintain a garden or keep outdoor plants, there are plenty of indoor plants that bring energy, oxygen, and a magical atmosphere into your home as well.

- **African Violet:** African violet can be used for love, friendship, and spirituality.
- **Aloe Vera:** Aloe vera's gel has many healing qualities, but aloe is also considered to be a very protective plant.
- **Anthurium:** Anthurium is a symbol of hospitality, but is also a sensual plant. Keep in your bedroom to keep lustful energy high.
- **Bay laurel:** Bay laurel does well in a container and can be grown indoors. A magical favorite for witches, bay leaves are used for protection, purification, healing, empowerment, wisdom, and wish spells.
- **Calathea:** Calathea helps initiate new beginnings and keep spirits happy in the home.
- **Christmas Cactus:** Cacti in general are protective plants and guard the house from negative energy and toxic influences. Christmas cactus also promotes kindness and generosity.

- **Chinese Money Plant:** This is a wonderful plant to have on hand to support prosperity and abundance in the home.
- **Cyclamen:** Cyclamen can be used in love spells.
- **English Ivy:** English ivy can be used for protection.
- **Orchids:** Orchids are used for love magic and to identify and feel your inner beauty.
- **Peperomia:** Peperomia has a grounding and earthy energy.
- **Philodendron:** Philodendron can help keep happiness high in your home.
- **Pothos:** Pothos can be used to help reach goals.
- **Snake Plant:** Snake plants awaken wisdom.
- **Spider Plant:** Spider plants conjure creativity and also protect the home from illness.

SELF-CARE SPELLCRAFTS FOR THE GREEN WITCH

You don't have to be a gardener or a wild-harvester to take advantage of the magic that the plant world has to offer. Many of the ingredients in the recipes below may already be in your kitchen, but all are widely available in metaphysical shops and online.

Here, you'll find several traditional spellcrafts, including incense, spell bottles, and herbal sachets. If there are ingredients you can't find, do some research (and use your intuition) to identify possible substitutions, and feel free to tweak any spell or recipe to tailor it more to your unique self-care needs.

LOOSE LEAF INCENSE FOR COURAGE

This is an incense that you can burn when you want to feel a sense of courage and empowerment. You can also use this blend to add extra power to a spell.

You will need:

- 2 tbsp. dragon's blood resin
- 2 tsp. dried rosemary

- 2 tsp. dried thyme
- 2 tsp. dried yarrow
- ½ tsp. ginger powder
- 7 drops cardamom essential oil

Instructions:

Crush all of the ingredients with a mortar and pestle so they are in smaller, finer pieces. Pour into a bowl. Add the cardamom oil and blend well.

Keep loose leaf incense in a sealed container.

SOLAR SUCCESS LOOSE LEAF INCENSE

This incense is blended together with flowers and herbs that are connected to the power of the sun. Use this incense when doing magic for strength, growth, success, and vitality.

You will need:

- 2 tsp. frankincense
- 2 tsp. grated and dried and orange peel
- 2 tsp. dried calendula
- 2 tsp. dried chamomile
- 2 tsp. nasturtium
- 2 crushed bay leaves
- 2 crushed sunflower petals
- ½ tsp. cinnamon

Instructions:

Crush the frankincense, bay leaves, and sunflower petals with a mortar and pestle until they are in smaller, finer pieces. Pour into a bowl and mix in the rest of the ingredients.

Keep loose leaf incense in a sealed container.

LOOSE LEAF INCENSE FOR PSYCHIC VISIONS

Use this incense when you are hoping to awaken your psychic senses. This is especially powerful for divination and channeling sessions.

You will need:

- 2 tbsp. frankincense resin
- 2 tsp. dried mugwort
- 1 tsp. dried lavender
- 1 tsp. dried lemongrass
- 1 tsp dried dandelion
- ½ tsp. cinnamon powder
- 1 bay leaf
- 6 drops sandalwood essential oil

Instructions:

Crush all of the ingredients, except for the cinnamon powder and bay leaf, with a mortar and pestle so they are in smaller, finer pieces.

Pour into a bowl and stir in the cinnamon powder. Crush the bay leaf and stir into the mix. Add the sandalwood oil and blend well.

Keep loose leaf incense in a sealed container.

SPELL BOTTLE TO EASE DEPRESSION

While spell bottles are traditionally said to be for protection, this spin on the tradition has a blend of herbal and crystal ingredients that will work as a charm to aid in easing depression. While it is always important to seek professional help when you need it, this little bottle can add some spiritual and energy support as well. Keep by your bedside to relieve depression. In a small jar or bottle, layer the following, in the order listed.

The amount of each ingredient listed below will depend on the size of container you're working with, but aim for enough so that a layer of each is visible from the outside of the jar or bottle.

You will need:

- Small jar or bottle
- Pink Himalayan rock salt
- Rose quartz crystal chips
- Lavender flowers
- Wild bergamot petals
- Rose petals
- Vervain flowers
- St. John's wort flowers
- Chamomile flowers
- Piece of yellow ribbon

Instructions:

Layer the ingredients in the bottle or jar in the order listed above. Seal it shut and tie the yellow ribbon around it. If you are extra crafty, make a braid or thread together yellow, green, and pale purple embroidery threads.

Hold the bottle in your hand and say the following incantation:

"May this bottle help me find peace; may it lift depression out of me. Healing energies of relief and wellness, may this spell bottle fill with me self-love and tenderness."

SPELL BOTTLE FOR THE HIGHLY SENSITIVE PERSON

Being sensitive can be an incredible gift: it can mean you are able to emphasize with others, read body language, pick up on the energy of a place, and be profoundly moved by emotional events. It can also feel a little overwhelming at times when the world is harsh and unfair. This spell bottle is meant to shield you from the negative energies of the outside world, all while purifying your space and reviving your sensitive traits, so you can feel at peace with your tender and gentle nature.

The amount of each ingredient listed below will depend on the size of container you're working with, but aim for enough so that a layer of each is visible from the outside of the jar or bottle.

You will need:

- Small jar or bottle
- Selenite crystal chips
- Aquamarine crystal chips
- Tulsi leaves and/or flowers
- Lavender buds
- Hyssop flowers
- Violet flowers
- Meadowsweet flowers

- A drop or two of helichrysum oil to top off the bottle

Instructions:

Layer the ingredients in the bottle or jar in the order listed above. Seal the jar shut and tie a pink or lilac colored ribbon around it.

Hold the bottle in your hand and say the following incantation:

"I am sensitive, I am soft, I am gentle. This is a gift and I am thankful to be this way. This bottle helps me move through the world at peace, and live with tender ease. As I will it, so mote it be."

PEACE AND LOVE BATH TEA

This combination of herbs is blended into a large bag to soak in bath water. The herbs in this tea are associated with deep relaxation, peacefulness, and attracting a mellow, wholesome, and loving vibe.

You will need:

- Large cotton muslin tea bag
- 2 tbsp. of each of the following dried herbs: chamomile, catnip, lavender, lemon balm, rose petals
- 2 cups Epsom salt
- Optional: If you have them on hand, gardenia fragrance oil and/or a couple drops of topical CBD oil are nice to add as well.

Instructions:

Add the herbs to the muslin bag and tie it shut. When you draw the bath, add the Epsom salt. Then add the muslin bag into the bath to soak with you.

Relax, focusing on allowing deep breaths and releasing any tension in your body and mind. Try to stay in the bath for at least 20 minutes.

SWEET DREAMS SLEEPING SACHET

This is a small pillow to fill with herbs that promote rest and pleasant dreams. If you are adept at sewing, you can make a small pillow using fabric with celestial night sky designs. Or, if you would rather keep it a little simpler, a deep purple or blue bag will work just fine.

You will need:

- Small pillow or drawstring bag (deep purple or blue)
- Equal amounts of the following herbs to fill the bag: mugwort, lavender, chamomile, hops, peppermint
- 3 drops each of the following essential oils: sandalwood, jasmine, lavender

Instructions:

Add the herbs to the bag or pillow and then blend in the oils, one at a time. Tie the bag (or sew the pillow) shut. Say the following incantation:

"Sweet dreams, psychic dreams, pleasant things appear to me!"

Take a moment to visualize yourself sleeping well, and imagine what the best dream you could have would look and feel like. Place the sachet or pillow under your regular pillow before going to sleep.

MAGICAL SACHET FOR SELF-ESTEEM

Carry this sachet with you when you are feeling like you need a little extra boost of self-esteem and goodwill towards yourself. You will need a peach, yellow, or orange bag.

You will need:
- Drawstring bag (peach, yellow, or orange)
- Equal amounts of the following herbs/dried flowers to fill the bag: chamomile, catnip, bee balm, daisies, yellow roses
- Piece of citrine
- Piece of mookaite
- 2 drops of each of the following essential oils: vetiver, geranium, bergamot

Instructions:
Add the herbs to the bag, then add the citrine and mookaite. Next, blend in the oils, one at a time. Tie the bag shut. Say the following incantation:

"I feel love and joy for myself. When I carry this bag, I feel my self-esteem burst with optimism and hope."

Keep the sachet with you for a few days, and take note of any differences in how you feel. Over time, you may want to periodically recharge your sachet by holding it in your hands and repeating the incantation above.

GET WELL SOON HEALING SACHET

This sachet is meant to be carried when working on healing the physical body. While it is not a replacement for seeking medical attention, it is a nice charm to carry to give an energetic and magical boost while in the process of healing.

This makes a very nice gift for someone who is feeling under the weather (with their permission). You will need a green pouch for this sachet.

You will need:

- Green drawstring bag or pouch
- Equal amounts of the following herbs to fill the bag: peppermint, thyme, rue, St. John's wort, chamomile, echinacea
- 1 piece aventurine
- 1 piece unakite
- 1 drop peppermint oil
- 1 drop eucalyptus oil

Instructions:

Add the herbs to the bag, then add the aventurine and unakite. Next, add the peppermint and eucalyptus oils and blend well. Seal the bag shut. Say the following incantation (Note: this incantation also applies to yourself, if you are the one in the process of healing.):

"Get well soon, my dear friend. This illness is coming to a quick end. Your health and energy will be restored again. May this bag carry the magical healing that I send."

If the sachet is for you, keep it with you until you're feeling better. If it's a gift, advise the recipient to do the same.

PROTECTIVE BOUNDARY POWDER

This powder can be ground up and scattered around your property, or another specific boundary where you would like to keep out negative influences, toxic energy, and threatening or low vibrations.

You will need:

- 1 part cayenne pepper
- 2 parts black pepper
- 2 parts sea salt
- 2 parts dried rosemary
- 2 parts dried hyssop
- 3 parts dragon's blood resin (use smaller pieces or grind finely)
- 3 parts soot and ashes from a cauldron or other fire
- 1 part dried rose stems (with needles), cut into fine pieces

Instructions:

Blend the cayenne pepper, black pepper, sea salt, rosemary, and hyssop together. Grind until it is a fine powder. Pour into a mixing container. Blend in the dragon's blood, soot and ashes, and dried rose stems.

Sprinkle the powder around the boundaries you're protecting. As you go, visualize an energetic wall rising up from the powder, surrounding your space with protection and infusing it with white light.

Chapter Six: INTUITIVE SELF-CARE: DIVINATION AND OTHER TOOLS TO DEEPEN YOUR PRACTICE

The art of divination is as old as recorded history. The ancients often read bones or sticks to assess future outcomes for the community, such as whether a good harvest was in store or the chances of success in battle.

Today, with our plethora of divination tools—Tarot and other oracle cards, runes, scrying mirrors, pendulums, etc.—people often read for themselves, to see what is happening beyond what they are able to observe in the present moment.

Many witches enjoy using one form of divination or another as a means to gain additional insight and clarification on situations that weigh heavily on their minds. However, the most successful divination is conducted from a neutral, centered place.

When we are highly anxious about an issue, we're unlikely to get clear answers, no matter what tools we're using. If you ever find yourself feeling *worse* about your situation while doing a reading, it's time to step back, do what you can to calm and center yourself, and return to the question once you're feeling more stable.

When practiced regularly, divination can also help us strengthen our own intuition, allowing us to discern our best choices by going within, without need for any external tools. We have a built-in divination system in the form of our "hunches" about people, places, and choices, and we also receive messages in our dreams.

This chapter will examine some well-known divination techniques as they apply to self-care and personal development, as well as tips for working with your own unique intuitive system for finding answers from the spirit world. As you pursue your individual path to self-care, you can use these internal and external tools to guide your decisions and discover more of your whole, authentic self.

WORKING WITH A PENDULUM

Simply put, a pendulum is a weighted object suspended on the end of a string. However, the modern pendulums we see in metaphysical shops typically take the form of a crystal or other stone attached to a silver chain.

As you work through this book, you may find a pendulum to be a wonderful tool to have by your side. Pendulums can be used to answer "yes" or "no" questions, determine whether chakras are out of balance, and even determine whether a food or supplement will be beneficial for your body's specific needs. Anyone can learn to use a pendulum, making it an accessible divination tool with many benefits.

- **Pendulum Basics:** To start using a pendulum, be sure you have a steady surface to rest your elbow on. Hold the top of the pendulum's chain between your thumb and forefinger, letting the crystal hang directly below. Wait for the pendulum to stop moving and settle into stillness. Then ask, "Show me 'yes.'" Note which way the pendulum moves. Next, ask, "Show me 'no.'" The pendulum should move in the opposite direction, or it may move side-to-side instead of in a circular motion. Once you understand what "yes" and "no" look like when the pendulum swings, test it with a question that you already know the answer to. If it answers correctly, you can start working with the pendulum. If it answers incorrectly, or doesn't move at all, you may need to cleanse it of any cloudy or unwanted energy, then start again. It's also possible that now isn't the right time to work with a pendulum (especially if you feel unclear yourself!), so you may need to come back to it later. Be sure to ask only what you really want to know the answer to. Again, if you're feeling anxious about your question, now is probably not the right time to ask.

- **Pendulum over objects:** While this is often applied to food and supplements, you technically could do this exercise over any object to see if it is healthy for you or not. In this example we will use a piece of food, but you can try this over divination tools, magical tools, even books or plants. Go to your refrigerator and pull out something you think is healthy. Hold the pendulum over the food item and ask, "Is this food good for my body?" You can even narrow down your questions and ask, "Will this food give me acid reflux?" Or, "Will this food make me feel full?" It's an interesting exercise to see which foods your pendulum approves of!

- **Pendulum over chakras:** This is easier to do with a friend, but you can also do it for yourself. Begin by asking the pendulum to assist in balancing chakras. Lie on your back on the floor, and hold the pendulum over each chakra, starting with the root and moving upwards. (If you're working alone, you may want to place a mirror alongside your head so you can see the pendulum above your crown chakra.) If the chakra is off balance, the pendulum will either move wildly (overactive chakra) or move very little (underactive/blocked chakra). One practice for balancing the chakras is to keep the pendulum over the chakra until it is moving in a steady, clockwise circle. If you do this, be sure to cleanse your pendulum afterwards by placing it in sea salt or letting it sit in the sun.

- **Pendulum for self-healing sessions:** If you have an area that you know is uncomfortable for you, see if pendulum healing can be an added support in your recovery. Ask the pendulum to help remove the discomfort and aid in healing. Hold it over the area that needs healing and allow the pendulum to continue moving. The healing session is done when the pendulum slows to a stop in its neutral position. As with chakra balancing, be sure to cleanse your pendulum afterwards by placing it in sea salt or letting it sit in the sun.

INTUITION EXERCISE: GREEN LIGHT/ RED LIGHT

We often hear that it is valuable to "listen to our intuition," yet it sometimes feels like a difficult thing to identify and practice. Intuition can be defined as that gut feeling we have that pulls us to do something or to push away from something. Intuition feels like an internal magnet: we feel instinctively drawn towards something, or instinctively repelled away from something.

You may feel intuitively inclined to spend time with a new person, or intuitively concerned that that person may not have your best intentions in mind. You may feel a strong pull to go to a certain event —and if you go, you may find that you discover something very profound as a result. In the same way, you may have a "bad feeling" about driving a certain road home—and by changing your direction, you avoid getting into a car accident.

It seems so easy, yet we all have found ourselves doubting our intuition. This exercise, which is adapted from *Intuition and Beyond* by Sharon A. Klinger, may help you better recognize what your intuition is telling you to do.

1. Close your eyes and center yourself, taking deep breaths and feeling comfortable and safe in your surroundings.

2. With your eyes closed, recall a choice you made that didn't feel right. This doesn't need to be anything terrible; it can be something as simple as going for a "quick trip" to the grocery store the day before Thanksgiving and then standing in line for 30 minutes. Think of how it felt when you made that choice. You may feel your gut pulling you backwards. Now visualize a traffic light glowing red. Hold it in your mind's eye for a moment, and then clear the memory and the vision.

3. Next, think about a choice you made that turned out very well. This could be something as simple as calling your friend at the right time, or the house you decided to buy (that fabulous pair of shoes works too!). Think about how it felt when you made that choice. You may feel your gut pushing you forwards. Now visualize a traffic light glowing green. Hold it in your mind's eye for a moment, and then clear the thought and vision.

4. Moving forward, the next time you have to make a decision on something, center yourself and think about one of the options. In your mind's eye, visualize the traffic light: – does it turn red, and/or do you feel pulled backwards? Or, does it turn green, and/or do you feel pulled forwards? Now do the same with the other option. Take note of how the decision turns out now that you're following your intuition.

WORKING WITH YOUR DREAMS

Dreams are powerful experiences that every human has throughout their lives. Many dreams are reflections of our subconscious thoughts and desires, while others can feel like they are otherworldly messages or premonitions.

Some people regularly have vivid dreams they can recall easily, while others struggle to remember what happened in their dream by the time they get their cup of coffee. When we learn to pay attention to our dreams, we can learn a lot about ourselves. Our dreams become a dialogue with the universe about our soul's deepest desires.

There are many ways to work with your dreams in order to better understand yourself, gain insight into your soul's purpose, and even receive psychic messages. The following practices can help you improve the quality of your dreams, and enhance your ability to recall and make sense of them.

- **Keep a dream journal:** Even if you only have two minutes to commit to jotting down notes, keeping a dream journal will help you remember your dreams. What's more, this enables you to review prior dreams to see if there are patterns or recurring themes that may be trying to tell you something. You may also discover that some dreams turned out to be psychic premonitions. Keep a journal and pen by your bed so you can write immediately when you wake up.

- **Practice dream recall when you wake up:** In addition to dream journaling, you can also walk through your dream in your mind when you wake up. If you wake up in the middle of a dream, see how it feels to "complete" the dream in your imagination.

- **Create a comfortable sleeping environment:** Get blackout curtains if your windows let in artificial light at night. Turn off all devices (or put them in airplane mode), and keep your bedroom reasonably tidy. Place a piece of citrine and a piece of amethyst under your pillow to promote cheerful dreams and restful sleep, and/or moonstone and sodalite by your bed. You can also try using the Sweet Dreams Sleeping Sachet from Chapter 5.

- **Use an oil diffuser:** One blend that is soothing and supportive for dreamwork is equal parts jasmine, sandalwood, cedarwood, frankincense, and lavender. You can also use any oils you find personally soothing.

- **Make bedtime tea:** There are plenty of great sleeping blends available, or you can make your own with calming, dream-supporting herbs like chamomile, dandelion, lavender, mugwort, passionflower, and peppermint.

- **Make a dreamy bedtime snack:** Foods high in vitamin B6 and tryptophan may actually enhance dreams. Before you go to bed, try having a small snack of almonds, cherries, bananas, sunflower seeds, pumpkin seeds, tofu, cheese, turkey, or tuna.

- **Try listening to binaural beats:** Binaural beats are recordings that play tones at two different frequencies—one in your left ear and one in your right, which has a calming effect on the mind. If you can comfortably wear headphones at night, search for binaural beat music made specifically for dreaming.

- **Pray or ask for dreams before going to bed:** If you have a question you want help with, ask for the answer to be revealed during the night's dreaming session. You can also ask for vivid dreams, or simply say a mantra like, "Tonight my dreams will be vivid and valuable. When I wake up, I will recall what happened and will know I gained wisdom from the experience."

PERSONAL DEVELOPMENT IN THE TAROT COURT CARDS

If you're familiar with the Tarot, you know that the Court Arcana can be some of the trickiest cards in the deck. However, we can learn a lot from these various royal archetypes. In readings, these 16 cards typically illuminate aspects of personality and character. They may represent actual people involved in a situation, but they often speak to the way people are behaving with respect to the situation, or to the personal qualities required in order to successfully navigate it.

Personal reflection is crucial to self-care, and the court cards can be useful guides to self-discovery. They can show us aspects of ourselves that we may not be conscious of, and/or offer examples of traits and approaches to life that will benefit us. These cards can also reflect stages of our personal journey when it comes to specific domains of experience: inspiration, creativity, and drive (Wands); emotion, psychic receptivity, and spiritual development (Cups); intellect, learning, and mental agility (Swords); and abundance, stability, and grounded action (Pentacles).

In this context, Pages represent younger people, who are just starting out in the realm of experience represented by the suit. Knights are more experienced in their respective realms, but are not always mature enough to know how to successfully channel their highly charged energy. The Queen is the feminine embodiment of alchemizing the progress of the earlier stages into lasting positive outcomes, while the King is seen as the masculine embodiment of maturity and mastery over a situation.

The descriptions below examine the personality traits of each court card, as well as its zodiac sign correspondences, its associated personality type on the Myers-Briggs Type Indicator (MBTI), and its associated stage of personal development within the domain of its suit. You'll also find suggestions for when and how to work with each archetype to improve your well-being and get more enjoyment out of life. As you read through these descriptions, ask yourself—which archetypes do you relate to, and which ones would you like to be a little more like?

Note: if you don't have a Tarot deck, you can find images of the cards online. Even if you do have a deck of your own, it can be fun to research various decks to see all the different visual interpretations of the court archetypes. You can print out images of the cards and affix them to a firm backboard, or draw your own—be as creative as you wish!

PAGE OF WANDS

The Page of Wands is excited, enthusiastic, creative, bold, cheerful, and childlike. This Page celebrates playfulness, self-discovery, and happiness. This card is associated with all Fire signs and the INFP personality. The

Page of Wands represents the stage of creative inspiration and the start of new projects.

Work with the Page of Wands if you are beginning a new project and need a creative boost. This Page will motivate you to try a new hobby or revisit a practice you may have neglected. Build a vision board with the image of the Page of Wands.

KNIGHT OF WANDS

The Knight of Wands is charming, social, dynamic, confident, and unpredictable. This Knight celebrates adventures, wild parties, and high energy opportunities. This card is associated with Sagittarius and the ENTP and ENFP personalities. The Knight of Wands represents the stage of taking risks, seeking adventures, and gaining wisdom from new experiences.

Work with the Knight of Wands if you want a little more excitement and extroverted social time in your life—this Knight will give you more courage and help you be more curious. Have an image of the Knight of Wands present when you are planning your next holiday, taking an impromptu road trip, or getting ready for a night out. Carry an image of the Knight of Wands when you are at a festival or in a new situation to help you remain energized and enthusiastic.

QUEEN OF WANDS

The Queen of Wands is passionate, dramatic, imaginative, charming, expressive, and ambitious. This Queen celebrates inspired creations and bright and bold self-expression. This card is associated with Aries and Leo, and the INFJ and INTJ personalities. The Queen of Wands represents the stage of deepening self-expression and artistic creativity.

Work with the Queen of Wands when you are learning to be more imaginative, expressive, and extravagant. Have her image out when you are hosting a dinner party, redecorating a room, or trying on new outfits. To deepen your creativity, use the imagery of the card to write a story about this Queen's life.

KING OF WANDS

The King of Wands is funny, outgoing, optimistic, intense, entertaining, generous, and warm. This King celebrates good times, entertaining others, and keeping energy cheerful. This card is associated with Aries and Leo, and the ENFJ and ENTJ personalities. The King of Wands represents the stage of creative and artistic maturation, and an awareness of your inner strengths.

Work with the King of Wands when you need a burst of creative and/or optimistic energy and support in developing confidence. Study his image and reflect on what is going well for you. Visualize your highest outcomes and accept that happiness can manifest in your life.

PAGE OF CUPS

The Page of Cups is sensitive, empathic, dreamy, romantic, tender, and affectionate. This Page celebrates Star and Indigo children, psychic abilities, and emotional depths. This card is associated with all Water signs and the

INFP and ISFP personalities. The Page of Cups represents the stage of spiritual or psychic beginnings and a time to rediscover emotions.

Work with the Page of Cups when you are examining your emotions, feeling moody and sensitive, or are exploring how spirituality can benefit your life. Carry an image of the Page of Cups when you attend a healing circle or are meditating. Keep an image of the Page of Cups with a new divination kit.

KNIGHT OF CUPS

The Knight of Cups is romantic, poetic, introspective, creative, idealistic, and hopeful. This Knight celebrates romance, sensuality, new love interests, and fantasies. This card is associated with Pisces and ENFP or ESFP personalities. The Knight of Cups represents the stage of emotional exploration, by seeking to understand one's feelings and discern the wisdom of the heart.

Work with the Knight of Cups when you want to feel more aware of your moods and feelings, want to have new romantic experiences in your life, or are working through an emotionally complex situation. Write a poem or letter while sitting with an image of the Knight of Cups, go on a long drive listening to your favorite emotional songs, or get involved with a humanitarian cause.

QUEEN OF CUPS

The Queen of Cups is loving, nurturing, psychic, receptive, kind, empathic, and imaginative. This Queen celebrates love, feelings, connections with others, and spirituality. This card is associated with Cancer and INFJ or ISFJ personalities. The Queen of Cups represents the stage of spiritual and emotional development where you are aware of your feelings, abilities, and desires.

Work with the Queen of Cups when you want to focus on being a balanced and centered empath. She will help you develop your intuitive abilities and also support you as you explore your fantasies. Keep her image nearby when you are doing psychic work or love spells.

KING OF CUPS

The King of Cups is charitable, intuitive, mystical, and considerate, with a high emotional intelligence. This King celebrates his intuition, the arts, and seeing others live well and joyously. This card is associated with Scorpio and ENFJ and ESFJ personalities. The King of Cups represents the stage of emotional and spiritual maturation, where you feel motivated by intuition and high vibrational spirituality.

Work with the King of Cups when you want to feel deep compassion and unity with others. Volunteer with or donate to your favorite non-profit organization, or become a supporter of the arts in your community.

PAGE OF SWORDS

The Page of Swords is intelligent, intellectual, careful, alert, and sneaky. This Page celebrates independent thinking, smart opinions, and studying new things. This card is associated with Air signs, especially Aquarius, and ISTP and INTP personalities. The Page of Swords represents the stage of intellectual beginnings and the discovery of new interests for study and research.

Work with the Page of Swords if you are about to start a course in a new topic or simply want to become more informed. When reading a research book, use an image of the Page of Swords as your bookmark, or write your next to-do-list around the image of the Page of Swords.

KNIGHT OF SWORDS

The Knight of Swords is eager, animated, talkative, witty, impatient, energetic, and active. This Knight celebrates deep conversations, solving puzzles or challenges, and taking action on good ideas. This card is associated with Gemini and ENTP and ESTP personalities. The Knight of Swords represents the stage of intellectual exploration through learning and conversation, and a time to turn thoughts into reality.

Work with the Knight of Swords when you need to take action on thoughts and plans that have so far only been spoken about. Carry an image of the Knight of Swords when you are engaging in philosophical discussions and developing your own thoughtful perspectives.

QUEEN OF SWORDS

The Queen of Swords is independent, insightful, honest, straightforward, strong willed, and an eloquent speaker. This queen celebrates brilliant and unique company, self-sufficiency, and the language arts. This card is associated with Libra and ISTJ and INTJ personalities. The Queen of Swords represents the stage of mental development through transitions, ultimately leading to liberation from challenging circumstances.

Work with the Queen of Swords when you need to heal from a painful situation, feel like you need encouragement to get through something alone, or want to feel heard. Use her image for protection spells or writing spells. Visualize her when you are seeking truth and understanding in challenging matters.

KING OF SWORDS

The King of Swords is a powerful advisor and respected leader who is commanding, rational, logical, diplomatic, and aloof. This King celebrates strong leadership, pragmatism, and calculated decision-making. This card is associated with Aquarius and ESTJ and ENFJ personalities. The King of Swords represents the stage of intellectual maturation and mental clarity, and becoming a respected thought leader.

Use an image of the King of Swords when you want to obtain respect for your work and your choices. Carry his image when you need to make difficult decisions that impact others. Share the research and knowledge you've acquired with others who are interested.

PAGE OF PENTACLES

The Page of Pentacles is quiet, reflective, diligent, practical, and fascinated with the world. This Page celebrates quiet time to learn, contemplate, and mindfully observe the world and its many wonders. This card is associated with Earth signs, especially Taurus, and ISFP and

ISTP personalities. The Page of Pentacles represents the stage of discovering new skills, vocations, and professional paths.

Use an image of the Page of Pentacles when you are applying for new jobs or learning a new practical skill. Carry the Page of Pentacles with you when working at an internship, or when you want a solitary day, free of interruptions, to observe the world around you.

KNIGHT OF PENTACLES

The Knight of Pentacles is reliable, stable, slow, practical, responsible, and hard-working. This Knight celebrates taking things slowly and pausing from action for rest and reflection before making the next move. This card is associated with Virgo and ESFP and ESTP personalities. The Knight of Pentacles represents the stage of exploring choices and considering options thoughtfully, so as to not make a mistake.

Carry an image of the Knight of Pentacles when you need solitary time to consider skills that would help develop success and abundance in your life. Keep the Knight of Pentacles with you if you are practicing active listening and working on growing more in your life.

QUEEN OF PENTACLES

The Queen of Pentacles is healing, caring, generous, sensual, materialistic, decadent, thoughtful, and maternal. This Queen celebrates the healing arts, living lavishly and taking care of others so they can feel as good as she does. This card is associated with Capricorn and Taurus, and ISFJ and ISTJ personalities. The Queen of Pentacles represents the stage of developing and honoring abundance and the ability to manifest beneficial outcomes while caring for others.

Carry an image of the Queen of Pentacles if you are a healer. Use her image in healing spells or keep her image visible when you want to invite a healthy support system into your life.

KING OF PENTACLES

The King of Pentacles is successful, responsible, dependable, self-sufficient, productive, and healthy. This King celebrates prosperity and abundance through dedicated and ambitious action. This card is associated with Capricorn and Taurus, and ESFJ or ESTJ personalities. The King of Pentacles represents the stage of professional maturation, when you feel stable and can provide stability for others.

Use an image of the King of Pentacles in abundance and prosperity magic, and/or keep this image in your wallet or place of business. Share your abundance with your friends, practice gratitude, and make physical healing and balancing money your priorities.

COURT CARD EXPLORATION SPREAD

This spread can be useful to try when you are reading about the court cards in this chapter and wish to better understand your motives and next steps. Before doing this spread, pull all the court cards from your deck and choose one that you believe represents you the best—the court card you relate to the most. Use that card to gauge where you feel presently. Then, shuffle the remaining court cards and draw three:

Card 1: You at Your Best: This card represents the next stages of development in your life. It shows you where to focus your attention and where you shine.

Card 2: Courtly Wisdom: This card represents a member of the court you can receive messages and wisdom from. This card can also represent lessons you may experience that mirror the lifestyle choices and preferences that would be made by this court member.

Card 3: Exemplification: This is a member of the court cards you should strive to be more like. What practical things would you do that this court member would also do?

CARD SPREADS FOR SELF-CARE

Whether you just want a quick check-in, or a full reading examining your self-care journey from multiple angles, divination spreads are great for connecting with your heart, mind, and spirit.

Here are a few different spreads to try out with your Tarot, oracle, or Lenormand cards. These spreads are also suitable for other casting divination tools such as the Ogham or runes.

SIMPLE CHECK-IN SPREAD

Use this simple three card spread to check in with yourself and see how you are doing at the present moment.

Card 1: Physical Check-In: How is your body feeling? How are you responding to the world around you? This card may show a way to feel more physically balanced.

Card 2: Mental Check-In: How are you feeling mentally? What is going on in your mind that you are focused on right now? This card may show you a way to have more ease in your thoughts.

Card 3: Spiritual Check-In: How are you feeling spiritually? What can you do to feel close to divinity? This card may show you ways to become more connected to your magical powers.

COMFORTING CARD SPREAD

Use this card spread when you are feeling stressed, anxious, and/or uncomfortable.

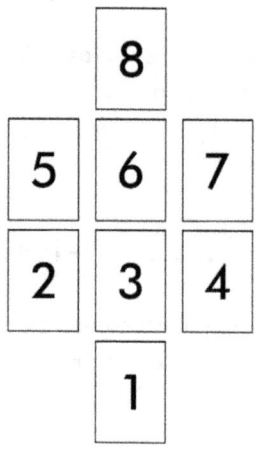

Card 1: Your current situation.

Card 2: The source of your stress, anxiety, and/or discomfort.

Card 3: How you define comfort. What comfort feels like to you, and what you believe would give you comfort presently.

Card 4: Something to focus on right now to begin turning your attention to balance, hope, and relaxation.

Card 5: Something that can bring you physical comfort—actions to take or practices to begin for comfort in your body and surroundings.

Card 6: Something that can bring you emotional comfort—actions to take or practices to begin for mental well-being and feelings of emotional relief.

Card 7: Something that can bring you energetic comfort—actions to take or practices to begin to ensure that you are energetically grounded, protected, and supported.

Card 8: A message, advice, or wisdom from your spirit guide.

SELF-AWARENESS SPREAD

This spread returns to the "self-words" examined in the introduction of this book. You can use this spread as a means to better understand where you are thriving and where you need to pay better attention. It is a great spread to use when you need direction.

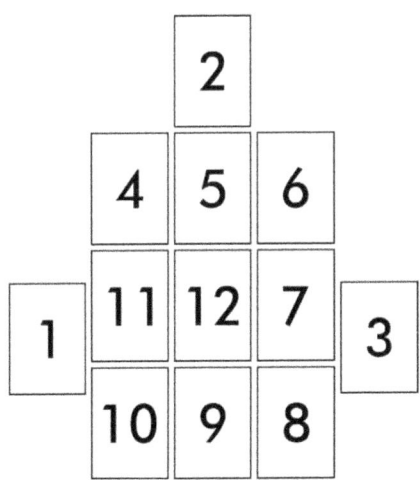

Card 1: Self-Talk: What is in your mind at the present moment—what is ruling your thoughts.

Card 2: Self-Gratitude: Something in your life you can currently be grateful for.

Card 3: Self-Seeking: Something you need to seek out in pursuit of a better understanding of your soul's purpose.

Card 4: Self-Development: Something worth developing in your life. A skill, hobby, or talent to focus on now.

Card 5: Self-Maintenance: Something that needs attention in your life. What aspect of your life needs maintenance at the moment?

Card 6: Self-Discipline: Where you need to practice control and remain disciplined.

Card 7: Self-Forgiveness: Something you need to forgive yourself for, and/or how to be more forgiving with yourself.

Card 8: Self-Esteem: How you regard yourself, and/or something that can authentically boost your self-esteem.

Card 9: Self-Love: Where you need to be more loving with yourself, and/or ways to show yourself more love.

Card 10: Self-Compassion: How to be more sensitive to your needs, or needs that are currently unmet. Methods for showing yourself more tenderness and kindness.

Card 11: Self-Expression: What you need to say, or a way to creatively express yourself.

Card 12: Self-Discovery: Lessons, events, and/or revelations you are experiencing or may encounter in the future.

CONCLUSION

As you know by now, self-care is as unique as the individual who is practicing it. Making the time and effort to focus on self-care can be life-altering in how you feel—both physically and magically.

When we turn our attention inwards and work on our own needs, we ultimately feel peace and tenderness with ourselves. This radiates into the world around us, giving us a direct spiritual connection to divinity.

My hope is that you will revisit this book often, and discover other books that help you to discover the ways you best like to take care of yourself. As you do, you will find that you are healthier, happier, more balanced, and able to manifest incredible opportunities for yourself.

SUGGESTIONS FOR FURTHER READING

Chakra Healing: A Beginner's Guide to Self-Healing Techniques that Balance the Chakras. Margarita Alcantara, 2017.

An Herbalist's Guide to Formulary: The Art & Science of Creating Effective Herbal Remedies. Holly Bellebuono, 2017.

A Goddess Is a Girl's Best Friend: A Divine Guide to Finding Love, Success, and Happiness. Laurie Sue Brockway, 2002.

Wicca Essential Oils Magic. Lisa Chamberlain, 2022.

Magical Aromatherapy: The Power of Scent. Scott Cunningham, 1989.

A Curious Future: A Handbook of Unusual Divination and Unique Oracular Techniques. Kiki Dombrowski, 2018.

Rosemary Gladstar's Medicinal Herbs: A Beginner's Guide. Rosemary Gladstar, 2012.

Angels, Spirit Guides & Goddesses: A guide to working with 100 divine beings in your daily life. Susan Gregg, 2018.

The Complete Illustrated Encyclopedia of Magical Plants. Susan Gregg, 2013.

The Encyclopedia of Stones, Revised Edition. Judy Hall, 2013.

Llewellyn's Complete Formulary of Magical Oils. Celeste Rayne Heldstab, 2012.

Wheels of Life: The Classic Guide to the Chakra System. Anodea Judith, 1999.

Moon Phase Astrology: The Lunar Key to Your Destiny. Raven Kaldera, 2011.

Aromatherapy for Beginners. Anne Kennedy, 2018.

Intuition & Beyond: A Step-by-Step Approach to Discovering Your Inner Voice. Sharon A. Klinger, 2011.

Crystal Magic: Mineral Wisdom for Pagans and Wiccans. Sandra Kynes, 2017.

The Essential Guide to Aromatherapy and Vibrational Healing. Margaret Ann Lembo, 2016.

How to Be Well: The 6 Keys to a Happy and Healthy Life. Frank Lipman M.D., 2018.

The Spirit Almanac: A Modern Guide to Ancient Self-Care. Emma Loewe and Lindsay Kellner, 2018.

Self-Esteem: A Proven Program of Cognitive Techniques for Assessing, Improving, and Maintaining Your Self-Esteem, 4th ed. Matthe McKay PhD, 2016.

The Witch's Book of Self Care: Magical Ways to Pamper, Soothe, and Care for Your Body and Spirit. Arin Murphy-Hiscock, 2018.

Self-Care for the Real World: Practical Self-care Advice for Everyday Life. Nadia Narain and Katia Narain Phillips, 2017.

The Modern Witchcraft Guide to Magickal Herbs. Judy Ann Nock, 2019.

A Kitchen Witch's World of Magical Food. Rachel Patterson, 2015.

The Complete Guide to Crystal Chakra Healing. Philip Permutt, 2008.

The Book of Stones: Who They Are and What They Teach, Revised Edition. Robert Simmons and Naisha Ahsian, 2015.

Herb Magic: An Introduction to Magical Herbalism and Spells. Patti Wigington, 2020.

Wellness Witch: Healing Potions, Soothing Spells, and Empowering Rituals for Magical Self Care. Nikki Van Der Car, 2019.

Magical Self-Care for Everyday Life. Leah Vanderveldt, 2020.

ABOUT THE AUTHORS

Kiki Dombrowski is an active member of the magical community as a teacher, writer, and divination reader. Kiki has a successful writing career, being a long-time writer for *Witch Way Magazine*, a featured writer in Lisa Chamberlain's annual datebook journals, and a co-author for *Witch Way's Book of 100 Love Spells*. Her book *A Curious Future* is a well-loved, critically acclaimed collection of unique and unusual divination techniques. Her newest book, *Transformative Tarot*, is about approaching tarot for self-development and spiritual exploration. Kiki has a BA in English and Creative Writing from Southern Connecticut University and a MA in Medieval Literature from Nottingham University. She has appeared as a guest on numerous popular podcasts, including the Witch Daily Show, Penny Royal Podcast, Conspirinormal, Pagan's Witchy Corner, and 6 Degrees of John Keel. For more information please visit **www.kikidombrowski.com**.

Lisa Chamberlain is the successful author of more than twenty books on Wicca, divination, and magical living, including *Green Witchcraft for Beginners*, *Wicca Book of Herbal Spells*, *Elemental Magic*, *Magic and the Law of Attraction, Runes for Beginners,* and *Tarot for Beginners.* An intuitive empath, she has been exploring witchcraft, magic, and other esoteric paths since her teenage years. Her spiritual journey has included a traditional solitary Wiccan practice as well as more eclectic studies across a wide range of belief systems. Lisa's focus is on positive magic that promotes self-empowerment for the good of the whole. You can find out more about her and her work at her website, **www.wiccaliving.com**.

THREE FREE AUDIOBOOKS PROMOTION

Don't forget, you can now enjoy **three audiobooks completely free of charge** when you start a free 30-day trial with Audible.

If you're new to the Craft, *Wicca Starter Kit* contains three of Lisa's most popular books for beginning Wiccans. You can download it for free at:

www.wiccaliving.com/free-wiccan-audiobooks

Or, if you're wanting to expand your magical skills, check out *Spellbook Starter Kit,* with three collections of spellwork featuring the powerful energies of candles, colors, crystals, mineral stones, and magical herbs. Download over 150 spells for free at:

www.wiccaliving.com/free-spell-audiobooks

Members receive free audiobooks every month, as well as exclusive discounts. And, if you don't want to continue with Audible, just remember to cancel your membership. You won't be charged a cent, and you'll get to keep your books!

Happy listening!

MORE BOOKS BY LISA CHAMBERLAIN

Wicca for Beginners: A Guide to Wiccan Beliefs, Rituals, Magic, and Witchcraft

Wicca Book of Spells: A Book of Shadows for Wiccans, Witches, and Other Practitioners of Magic

Wicca Herbal Magic: A Beginner's Guide to Practicing Wiccan Herbal Magic, with Simple Herb Spells

Wicca Book of Herbal Spells: A Book of Shadows for Wiccans, Witches, and Other Practitioners of Herbal Magic

Wicca Candle Magic: A Beginner's Guide to Practicing Wiccan Candle Magic, with Simple Candle Spells

Wicca Book of Candle Spells: A Book of Shadows for Wiccans, Witches, and Other Practitioners of Candle Magic

Wicca Crystal Magic: A Beginner's Guide to Practicing Wiccan Crystal Magic, with Simple Crystal Spells

Wicca Book of Crystal Spells: A Book of Shadows for Wiccans, Witches, and Other Practitioners of Crystal Magic

Tarot for Beginners: A Guide to Psychic Tarot Reading, Real Tarot Card Meanings, and Simple Tarot Spreads

Runes for Beginners: A Guide to Reading Runes in Divination, Rune Magic, and the Meaning of the Elder Futhark Runes

Wicca Moon Magic: A Wiccan's Guide and Grimoire for Working Magic with Lunar Energies

Wicca Wheel of the Year Magic: A Beginner's Guide to the Sabbats, with History, Symbolism, Celebration Ideas, and Dedicated Sabbat Spells

Wicca Kitchen Witchery: A Beginner's Guide to Magical Cooking, with Simple Spells and Recipes

Wicca Essential Oils Magic: A Beginner's Guide to Working with Magical Oils, with Simple Recipes and Spells

Wicca Elemental Magic: A Guide to the Elements, Witchcraft, and Magical Spells

Wicca Magical Deities: A Guide to the Wiccan God and Goddess, and Choosing a Deity to Work Magic With

Wicca Living a Magical Life: A Guide to Initiation and Navigating Your Journey in the Craft

Magic and the Law of Attraction: A Witch's Guide to the Magic of Intention, Raising Your Frequency, and Building Your Reality

Wicca Altar and Tools: A Beginner's Guide to Wiccan Altars, Tools for Spellwork, and Casting the Circle

Wicca Finding Your Path: A Beginner's Guide to Wiccan Traditions, Solitary Practitioners, Eclectic Witches, Covens, and Circles

Wicca Book of Shadows: A Beginner's Guide to Keeping Your Own Book of Shadows and the History of Grimoires

Modern Witchcraft and Magic for Beginners: A Guide to Traditional and Contemporary Paths, with Magical Techniques for the Beginner Witch

FREE GIFT REMINDER

Just a reminder that Lisa is giving away an exclusive, free spell book as a thank-you gift to new readers!

Little Book of Spells contains ten spells that are ideal for newcomers to the practice of magic, but are also suitable for any level of experience.

Read it on read on your laptop, phone, tablet, Kindle or Nook device by visiting:

www.wiccaliving.com/bonus

DID YOU ENJOY
SELF-CARE FOR WITCHES?

Thanks so much for reading this book! I know there are many great books out there about Wicca, so I really appreciate you choosing this one.

If you enjoyed the book, I have a small favor to ask—would you take a couple of minutes to leave a review for this book on Amazon?

Your feedback will help me to make improvements to this book, and to create even better ones in the future. It will also help me develop new ideas for books on other topics that might be of interest to you. Thanks in advance for your help!

www.ingramcontent.com/pod-product-compliance
Lightning Source LLC
Chambersburg PA
CBHW060108230426
43661CB00003B/117